BULLY PROOF

Handling harassment at work

Jean Kelly

Published by
aurora books
3a Lower James Street
LONDON
W1R 3PN
Email: Aurorabk@aol.com

ISBN 0 9535314 0 6

Designed and Produced by
Axxent Ltd
St Stephen's House
Arthur Road
Windsor
Berkshire, SL4 1RY

For Louise and Laura

Contents

Acknowledgements

I would like to thank the many people I have had the privilege of working with, either as colleagues, clients or friends. Without the wealth of their experiences, this book would have been impossible.

I would also like to thank my Neuro-Linguistic Programming teachers, including Sue Knight, Ian Ross and Gene Early, whose influence on my work has been considerable.

I wish to give credit and recognition to John Grinder and Richard Bandler, co-developers of NLP, and to Robert Dilts for contributing so much to the field of NLP.

I have given references where I can to the stories that feature in this book. I heard the story *Hell and Heaven* on an NLP training course by Sue Knight Associates. Stephen Serpell kindly gave me his version of *A Jewish Search.* The others I believe are generally known.

I would like to thank Sally Bryant for her advice and help at every stage of writing this book.

Above all, my special thanks go to my husband, Tom, for his never-ending support, encouragement and belief in my work.

Introduction

We are all harassed or bullied at some time in our lives, or witness friends and workmates being badly treated by others. Either as children or as adults at work, most of us have been on the receiving end of unreasonable and unwanted behaviour from peers, managers, colleagues or, indeed, friends.

This harassing or bullying behaviour takes many forms, including:

- Physical or verbal abuse
- Being humiliated or threatened in front of others
- Being set unreasonable deadlines or given excessive workloads
- Being the target for other people's humour or malice.

We can be subjected to this behaviour because of our gender, race, age, disability, or because we just happen to be the person the bully selects as a target.

Sometimes we may feel powerless to deal with this abuse, or find if we do react that the behaviour intensifies. We may report it to others only to discover we are not being taken seriously and nothing is being done about it. At other times we may introduce a defence mechanism by ignoring the bullying behaviour, or by not putting ourselves in a position where we will be subjected to such treatment in the first place.

Occasionally, the strategies we adopt are successful in preventing or stopping the harassment or bullying. We emerge from the situation feeling good about ourselves and confident in dealing with difficult relationships. We observe others suffering in their working relationships and find it hard to understand why they allow themselves to be treated so badly.

Often, though, this is not the case. Instead:

- We wonder why we are unable to challenge certain behaviour at work.
- We endure unpleasant behaviour for a long time and slowly it wears us down.
- There is one incident that leaves us hurt and powerless and this feeling can last many years.

BUT rather than putting up with being bullied or harassed we can all become bully proof by taking back the power in our relationships. You do not have to put up with this unpleasantness if you don't want to. If you would like to learn successful strategies in dealing with bullying or harassment or help your staff or colleagues to do so, then this book is for you.

As you read, you will learn how to:

- Make empowering changes so that you do not become or remain a victim to a harasser or bully.
- Adapt successful strategies other people have used to stay on course, believing in themselves, despite being faced with harassment and bullying.
- Develop a model that is right for you so that you can challenge the harasser or bully.

And by working through the exercises at the end of each chapter you will fully develop your ability to become **bully proof**.

Chapter 1

Sink or Swim

We all know that **sexual** and **racial harassment** can have an insidious and far-reaching effect in the world of work. Academic and organisational research during the 1990s in both the UK and the USA revealed the extent of this discriminatory abuse of power over employees in both the public and private sectors of employment. It is estimated that between 30% and 70% of female employees are, or have been, on the receiving end of unwanted behaviour of a sexual nature at work. The higher percentages are attributed to women working in male-dominated workplaces such as the army or the police.[1]

Bullying is an established feature of school life, but it has recently been recognised that bullying at work is also widespread. As with harassment, bullying involves a misuse of power. Employees may be intimidated or abused by managers or peers and made to feel isolated and vulnerable. Unlike harassment, bullying does not necessarily involve discrimination – anyone, woman or man, black or white, can be bullied at work or indeed be the bully. The bully may be a colleague, but in the vast majority of cases is more likely to be a manager or supervisor.[2]

---

[1] For definitions of all forms of harassment and bullying, and examples of what constitutes these forms of behaviour, see Appendix.

[2] The author's unpublished research in a Government department suggests that the bully is four times more likely to be a line or senior manager than a peer of the person claiming they are being bullied. This figure refers to employees who have not reported the bullying for fear of reprisals by the alleged bully.

As awareness grows of harassment and bullying at work, some responsible employers have developed policies and procedures in an attempt to deal with unacceptable behaviour. Staff and managers are trained to implement the policies and confidential advisers or counsellors are appointed to help people cope with unwanted conduct by fellow workers, clients and customers.

Employment tribunals take cases of harassment very seriously and occasionally have awarded six figure sums to employees who have been harassed. Wise employers realise they can be vicariously liable for the actions of their employees. They are keen to create a harmonious working environment and to ensure they are not called upon to defend themselves from embarrassing claims of harassment.

These cases do not only involve the costs of fines and legal fees. If you add expensive management time spent in investigating claims of harassment and the loss of productivity due to the sickness and absence of staff, unacceptable behaviour in the workplace can be very costly.

Yet, despite the growing awareness of the effects of harassment and bullying at work and the development of policies to tackle this sensitive subject, only a small proportion of cases is reported.[3]

There are many reasons for this. Staff may:

- be too frightened of the consequences of coming forward
- suspect they will not be believed or will lose their jobs as a result of complaining
- think they are somehow at fault
- know that others have complained of similar incidents and nothing was done to improve matters

[3] According to research by the Andrea Adams Consultancy, only 16% of people who have been bullied say they would approach their Personnel Department for help.

- prefer to shut up and put up with it
- as a last straw, leave the organisation.

Policies and procedures may be in place, but they alone are not usually enough to encourage staff to report unacceptable behaviour or to tackle it for themselves. Raising awareness of harassment and bullying at work is an important first stage in creating the corporate cultural change needed if all employees are to be treated with dignity. We all have a basic human right to respect, no matter where we are located in the organisational hierarchy. And companies have a legal responsibility to ensure that harassment and bullying at work are not taking place.[4]

Effective policies and procedures are paramount in laying the foundations for change in this sensitive area. To make it clear that harassment and bullying are unacceptable, these policies need senior management endorsement and staff well trained in the procedures.

Yet, despite the attempts of caring and well-meaning employers, it remains a major step for recipients of abuse to complain about a manager or a fellow worker or to seek help from the company.

The key spokes in the wheel of change are missing. Meaningful change will not occur as long as the recipients of harassment and bullying continue to have victim identities and to believe they are powerless, or incapable of challenging unacceptable behaviour at work.

Unless employees feel resourceful enough to have the confidence to deal with unacceptable behaviour at work, fundamental and lasting change will not take place. Anything an organisation does, however well meaning, is only the aspirin for the headache. It does not deal with the cause of the pain, or prevent it from recurring. For this workplace 'illness' to be irradicated, **the recipients of harassment need to heal themselves or bolster their immunity to the disease.**

[4] For an overview of discrimination law and harassment and bullying, see Appendix.

Already, I can hear the protests that we cannot allow the 'victims' to be unprotected and to deal with this problem unsupported; that it is the company's responsibility to combat harassment. Certainly, companies must not ignore their legal or social responsibilities. However, this should not prevent them from having a strong commitment to empowering individual employees to feel good about themselves in the context of challenging unacceptable behaviour at work.

Power is the key factor. When someone is harassed or bullied, or if they encounter conflict with team members or customers, they feel their power has been taken away, or the alleged perpetrator has used his or her powerful status against them. If the organisation then steps in and sorts out the problem, this can reinforce the fact that the person who was bullied or harassed was a victim waiting to be helped.

Why be a victim?

> ***If there is a hell on earth, living as a victim with feelings of anger and blame defines it. If there is a heaven on earth, living powerfully and lovingly as the creator of our own lives defines it.*** [5]

A victim is someone who suffers harm from another and feels wretched and powerless. There are times when we may become victims of, for example, violent crime or road accidents; instances when we do indeed suffer and may be unable to help ourselves.

If you are on the receiving end of harassment and bullying at work, you may feel powerless, wretched and paralysed into inaction by the misery of the situation. It may seem like the bullies, harassers and, sometimes, the organisation itself are robbing you of your feeling of self worth and encouraging you to take on a victim-like stance.

---

[5] Susan Jeffers, *End the Struggle and Dance with Life*, Hodder and Stoughton, London, 1997. Reproduced by permission of Hodder and Stoughton Limited.

However, as soon as this 'victim mentality' takes over, you lose even more of your power and control. In a sense, you are saying to the bully or harasser, "Here I am, bully me. After all, I am only a poor soul."

> *Jim, a professional working in a Government department, told me how his boss bullied him. "I had a terrible time with this woman. At first, we worked quite well together, but I think at some level she was threatened by me, as I was more qualified than she was. She began continually to criticise my work. She made it clear to me that it would take me two years to complete a piece of work that others would do in six months. She was right. The victim came out in me and, although I didn't deliberately underachieve, I was demotivated and took much longer to do the work than I should have."*

Jim's boss exploited her power over him. Her constant criticism and poor management caused him much distress. However, at some level, Jim recognised that he had allowed his boss to turn him into a victim. He gave away his power to her. Although he was a well-qualified specialist in a senior position, he recognised that he had allowed this woman to browbeat him into failure.

By becoming a victim, he played directly into her hands. And once he gave away his power and became a victim, this allowed his boss to bully him even more. By taking on a victim mentality, Jim influenced the behaviour of his boss. He had a direct impact on her. She became stronger as Jim became weaker.

Who do we allow to steal our power from us at work?

- Managers are the obvious people we give our power to. We may allow them to treat us with disrespect, or to tyrannise us with their criticism and threats.
- Sometimes, we give our power to colleagues or groups of colleagues. We let them pick on us, boss us around, tease us and even verbally and physically abuse us.

- We give our power to the organisations we work for. This enables them to step in and sort out our problems for us, or ignore our wishes and trample on our feelings.

As employees, we have a right to be treated with dignity and respect. However, we also have a responsibility to act in a way that inspires this respect and to state when we feel we are not receiving it. If we allow ourselves to become paralysed victims of others' power and, in so doing, do not challenge unacceptable behaviour, we are allowing others to take away our power.

Organisations, by relying solely upon using their policies and procedures to 'help' the 'victim' of harassment and bullying, are taking on a caretaking role. Individually, we each have a part to play in dealing with harassment and bullying – either on our own behalf or that of our colleagues. By giving all the power to the organisation to combat harassment and bullying we are compounding our victim-like stance or that of our colleagues.

We give away our power when we take on a victim-like stance in response to harassment or bullying. It is essential to recognise this if we are to take back control. Likewise, if we are training or supporting staff in our organisation, it is vital they understand this point.

A friend told me that she was on a canoeing holiday with her husband in France. "We had a canoe each," she said. "It was his fault I found it hard at first. He made me paddle round and round in circles."

"How did he do that," I asked, "if you were in different boats?" My friend started to laugh when she realised what she had said.

In a bullying or harassment situation, are you allowing the bully or harasser to take away your power? Are you becoming browbeaten, humiliated or stressed by their actions? If so, how are they doing that to you? How have you allowed them to have this power over you? To answer these questions, begin by answering the next one.

Ask yourself what benefit you derive from giving away your power?

This may seem a contradiction in terms. How can anyone 'benefit' from being a victim? Surely no one wants to feel like this?

Think about my friend in the example above. What benefit did she gain from blaming her husband for her poor canoeing performance? Could it be that she was able to believe one or more of the following?

- It was her husband's fault she didn't canoe well, not hers.
- If he hadn't been there, she might have been an excellent canoeist.
- Left to herself she would have been a good canoeist instantly.
- He was a typical husband – taking over and bossing her about. No wonder she made a mess of it.

So the benefit she derived from blaming her husband was that she didn't have to admit she was a poor canoeist – or at least a novice canoeist.

So let's apply this thinking to harassment and bullying situations. By taking on a victim role, perhaps you or your colleagues benefit in one or all of the following ways:

- You feel safe not challenging the more powerful person.
- You get sympathy from others.
- You don't fail – it is the other person who is in the wrong.
- You are a poor soul and people will protect you.
- You don't have to take responsibility for your own actions – someone else will sort things out, or, if they don't, it won't be your fault.

This may sound harsh. After all, in many cases of harassment and bullying the perpetrators are senior staff and the recipients of the unwelcome behaviour are junior in age or status. Taking on a victim role may appear to be the only way to survive in that situation, or the safest thing to do. It is important to recognise that we each have our own ways of looking after ourselves and doing what is right for us in every circumstance, even if others would do something differently.

However, the key point here is that by choosing to be a victim, we are fulfilling a survival need. And this is a choice we have made. **In many situations, we could choose to do something else.** Instead of sinking in a sea of misery, we can learn to swim to happier shores.

> *Margaret was a member of the senior management team reporting to one of the senior directors. "He bullied all his staff," she told me. "He strutted around the office like a dictator. We were all frightened of him – even those of us in the senior team. But some days, instead of letting him browbeat me, I would turn his behaviour into a joke. For example, he would snap his fingers at me in the corridor to attract my attention, instead of using my name. So I would make a comment such as, "Have you lost your dog, John?" He'd always laugh when I reacted towards him this way and on those occasions the atmosphere became less fearful."*

We need to recognise that there are times in our lives when bullying or harassment may be more likely to happen to us. These times could include occasions when we are already feeling stressed or unhappy by events in our personal lives. Divorce, death in the family, or long term illness fit into this category. When we are at the end of our tethers, bullying or harassment at work can compound this victim mentality, or at least cause us to feel very vulnerable and unsure of ourselves.

> *Pauline told me how she was feeling very low after the death of her mother. "Our new manager seemed to take a dislike to me. I felt very tearful after my mother died and he enjoyed picking on me and criticising me in front of the others. The women on the section seemed to take his side. I knew he was egging them on to join in the nastiness. They would be whispering when I came into the room and then go quiet and ignore me. They would talk across me and leave me out of*

> *conversations. On one occasion they put a transfer notice on my desk. I tried to cope with it all, but in the end I moved to another section."*

Vulnerability in other parts of our lives may add to our victim status. The bullies or harassers cleverly realise who is the 'weak' one in the team or organisation. They are unlikely to pick on the strongest, most senior person, and if they can find someone who is already weak, how much easier it is for them to bully or harass. If we find ourselves on the receiving end of bullying or harassment at a time when we are already struggling with big issues in our lives, then it is important for us to seek help or support from colleagues, Personnel, Human Resources, trades union or friends. In this way we give ourselves a better chance of not slipping into a victim-like position.

The realisation that there are times when we give away our power and that we do this for reasons of safety or comfort is very important. By understanding this, we can begin to ask ourselves what we are deriving from adopting a victim-like stance. We may decide we prefer to remain in the safety of being a victim, or we may decide we would rather assume control in our lives and become **bully proof**.

The choice is ours and it is crucial to realise that we have this choice. The purpose of this book is to help you find it.

> ***"What difference does it make?" Alice Walker responds, when asked about the discrimination she has faced as a black writer. "I do what I do and they do what they do. My work is to create and theirs is to attack. I prefer mine."[6]***

[6] Alice Walker quoted in *The Guardian*, 29th April, 1998.

Autobiography in Five Chapters[7]

Chapter One
I walk down the street.
There is a deep hole in the pavement.
I fall in.
I am lost … I am hopeless.
It isn't my fault.
It takes forever to find a way out.

Chapter Two
I walk down the same street.
There is a deep hole in the pavement.
I pretend I don't see it.
I fall in again.
I can't believe I'm in the same place.
But it isn't my fault.
It still takes a long time to get out.

Chapter Three
I walk down the same street.
There is a deep hole in the pavement.
I see it is there.
I still fall in … it's a habit.
My eyes are open.
I know where I am.
It is my fault.
I get out immediately.

Chapter Four
I walk down the same street.
There is a deep hole in the pavement.
I walk around it.

Chapter Five
I walk down another street.

[7] By Portia Nelson, quoted in C.L. Whitfield, *Healing the Child Within*, Health Communications, Orlando, Florida, 1989.

Exercise 1	**Taking back the power**
List the times when you felt and behaved like a victim. *e.g. When my boss criticised my work and behaviour at a meeting.* 1. 2. 3.	
Describe the impact your behaviour had on others. *e.g. I was tearful and angry. People felt sorry for me. This made me feel even more a poor soul.* 1. 2. 3.	
Describe the way a POWERFUL YOU would have behaved in this situation. *e.g. I could have spoken to my boss after the meeting, when I had got control of my emotions, and explained clearly how his behaviour had made me feel. Even if he had not apologised, I would have come out of the situation with dignity and power in the eyes of my colleagues. I think they would have supported me in doing this.* 1. 2. 3.	

Exercise 2	**On being powerful**

List times in the future when you will want to feel powerful.
e.g. When I begin my new role as assistant manager, I want to appear calm and reassuring to my staff.

1.

2.

3.

What impact do you think this POWERFUL YOU will have on others?
e.g. My staff will respect me and in return realise I respect them. This will create a situation where we can all discuss work-related matters together frankly and amiably.

1.

2.

3.

Chapter 2

Riding the Waves of Change

In the previous chapter we established that one of the options we have when reacting to harassment or bullying at work or unpleasant behaviour from colleagues or managers is to take on a victim-like stance. Sometimes this may seem to be the safest option. However, this approach may leave us feeling humiliated, bitter and powerless and incapable of taking purposeful and effective action.

We also saw that when those of us on the receiving end of abuse or criticism are also subject to change in our personal circumstances, such as divorce or a death in the family, we are particularly vulnerable to the powers of the bully or harasser. It is as if a traumatic change in one area of our lives makes unacceptable behaviour in another area more likely to happen or lessens our ability to deal with it.

Managing conflict and managing change are, therefore, inextricably linked. Change often brings about conflict and dealing with conflict involves managing change.

An example of this is when a new manager is appointed to a section. She or he introduces changes in working procedures and new ideas on how things should be done. We can feel very threatened by the 'new broom' and resent changing our way of doing things. This resentment can generate conflict with the new boss that may then lead to more changes. For example, we may find the new manager lessens our responsibilities, or heaps excessive workloads on to us.

So, if change itself can bring about conflict, what personal changes can we make to ensure we deal with conflict in a powerful and resourceful way? What changes are within our control?

One of the most important things to remember at this stage is:

> ***You cannot change another person. But you can change your reactions to them.***

Bearing this in mind can save us a great deal of anguish and frustration. How often in life have we thought we could change someone else? A partner, a teenager, an elderly parent? How hard we may have tried and with so little success. Those of us with children know that no matter how often we tell them to tidy up their rooms they ignore us and continue to leave their clothes and possessions lying around the floor. It is not easy to change them into the tidy individuals we wish them to be.

At work, too, we may try hard to change a member of our team, a colleague or a boss. We explain how we prefer a task to be done, but they continue to do it their way. We tell them again, but they carry on regardless.

This brings into mind the saying:

> ***Never try to teach a pig to sing. It wastes your time; and it annoys the pig.***[8]

How much time have we wasted and how much annoyance have we caused? And how little control have we had over the other person. All because we want to make someone behave and think as we do.

One way of retaining our power is to change that which we do have control over – our reactions. Instead of trying to change another person, if we change our reactions to them **we remain in control**. Instead of expecting them to change, we change

[8] An unknown sage quoted in Susan Jeffers, *End the Struggle and Dance with Life,* Hodder and Stoughton, London, 1997. Reproduced by permission of Hodder and Stoughton Ltd.

what we do in response to them. By so doing, we remain powerful and determined – neither a victim to their will, nor powerless in the face of their actions. This, in turn, may well result in a change in the behaviour of the other person.

After all, if you do what you always do, you get what you always got. So think about doing something differently and watch what happens.

> *"My manager's unpleasant behaviour towards me started as soon as I moved into his section. Week after week he would call me into his office, shut the door and stand in front of it while he ranted and raved at me – criticising my work in a personal and offensive way. I felt trapped. I wanted to crawl away and cower in a corner. One day, as he was shouting at me in his office, he moved away from the door. So I picked up my bag and walked out. I didn't say a word. I just walked out. This made a big impression on him. I couldn't say he was pleasant towards me after that, but he stopped bawling at me and began to talk to me in a normal voice."*

In the above example, by changing her reaction to her manager's abusive behaviour, Neena took back the power she had given to her manager. By walking calmly from the room, she showed him she could decide for herself whether she was prepared to subject herself to his unpleasantness. She made it clear that his behaviour was unacceptable to her and that she would not tolerate it. Neena threw off the victim stance she had assumed in her previous encounters with her boss and **the change in her reaction led to a change in his behaviour.**

A school in Teddington, West London, has introduced a buddying system to help younger students cope with potential bullies. The key to their coping is the changes they can make for themselves. As one buddy, an older student, explained, "The system provides support for younger students and gives them confidence. This really helps them because they are less likely to be picked on if they do not look vulnerable."

At school, children can learn that a change in how they react to other students can lead to a change in other people's behaviour towards them. **By becoming more confident with the help of their buddy, they lessen the chance of being a target for the bullies.** What a simple concept to learn and how valuable this will be to them as they grow up and become workers.

They will also have learned that support from their friends and peers is vital in this change process. As managers, team leaders, trainers and colleagues, we each have a role to play in creating workplaces free of harassment and bullying. No one should feel alone when faced with bullying or harassing behaviour. By supporting our colleagues and encouraging their growth in confidence we are beginning a change process which will make each and every one of us less vulnerable to bullies.

> *"I used to feel very uneasy in my relationship with a member of my team," said Kieran. "I tried to be respectful in the way I treated Jill, but she reacted very unpleasantly at the slightest criticism I made of her work. Over a period of time, I became quite anxious about having to reprimand her because of the outbursts she was capable of.*
>
> *"It wasn't until my colleague Josh pointed out how weak I appeared when she was around that I realised I needed to change my reaction to her. Josh told me how he had always had a good working relationship with Jill and, although he realised she was a fairly outspoken person, he did not find this daunting.*
>
> *"So I began to speak to her in a firm and assertive manner and made it clear I was no longer intimidated by her. This change in my attitude worked wonders. Jill has been sweetness and light towards me since. In fact, I am relieved at the change in the atmosphere at work now."*

From Kieran we learn that a change in our reaction to the behaviour of other people can cause them to change towards us. However, there is another important lesson to learn from

Kieran's situation. Josh, his colleague, recognised that Jill was a strong personality who would speak up for herself when she thought it was necessary. But unlike Kieran, he did not find this intimidating. Although Kieran and Josh were subject to similar behaviour from Jill, it was Kieran who became anxious about this. It was Kieran who found this behaviour **unwelcome and unwanted**.

In harassment and bullying situations it is important to recognise that one person may find a colleague's or manager's behaviour unwanted, but another person may not object to it at all. Workplace sexual and racial harassment policies should clearly explain this point.[9]

Everyone has the right to be treated with respect and dignity. If one person believes they are not being treated in this manner, they are entitled to challenge the behaviour or report it to a member of staff who can support them. It does not matter if everyone else in the section or team is prepared to tolerate the behaviour, or does not find it offensive. If one person finds it unwelcome and unwanted then the employer is obliged to listen to them and, if appropriate, take action.

Women and men may view what constitutes sexual harassment very differently. What may appear acceptable behaviour to a group of men may not be acceptable to a group of women. Joke telling and pin ups are obvious examples of this, as indeed are touching, fondling and unwelcome physical proximity. However, if we generalise about how women react or men react we will not reach firm conclusions either. A man may find sexual innuendo offensive whereas a woman may be happy joining in the joking. We are all individuals who see things differently from one another.

Bullying behaviour may also have a different impact on a woman than on a man. In some situations, bullying by a man of a woman may be construed as sexual harassment.

---

[9] See Appendix.

An employment tribunal held that a male manager who bullied female staff in particular unlawfully discriminated on the grounds of sex. A customer service administration manager claimed that she was forced to resign because of the personal and insulting remarks her manager often made in public about her work and attitude and that this amounted to sex discrimination.

The company tried to establish that although the manager behaved in a ruthless way he was equally ruthless towards the men and women who worked for him. However, the employment tribunal found that he bullied female staff in an unacceptable manner and that the greater proportion of his public rebukes and generally disparaging remarks were directed against the female staff. This, said the tribunal, amounted to sex discrimination and not the generally poor managerial attitude the company had held it to be.

Understanding what constitutes unwanted behaviour and the effect it has on individuals is a complex issue. It is vital to view the behaviour from the perception of the person on the receiving end of it. If the conduct is acceptable to you and I but unwanted by one of our colleagues, then we should try to understand their point of view. We need to step into their shoes and try to see what it feels like to be in their position. The reality they are experiencing may be very different from ours. We saw an example of how this can happen in the case of Kieran and Josh above. **Each of us is unique. We see and experience the world in our own way.**

We have established that one of the key changes we can make is to change our reaction to another person. We cannot change another person – but we do have control over our own reactions to them. By changing our reactions to unacceptable behaviour, we are taking back the control we may have given to the other person. We are throwing off the victim stance and proving we have power over our own behaviour.

A second change we can make centres around our perception of reality. **We have the power to alter our perception of reality.**

By so doing we have changed our reality as reality is only our perception of it. One definition of reality[10] is 'the state of things as they *appear* to be' and **we are all experts in changing how things appear to be**. We may have lost the knack or forgotten we had it, but as children we were adept at altering our concept of reality. As infants, how many of us believed there were monsters under our beds, or that an imaginary friend really existed? And how sure we were that we were right!

> *Louise came home from her first class at infant school singing, "I am the Lord of the dance settee."*
>
> *"You mean, 'Lord of the Dance, said he'," corrected her mum.*
>
> *But Louise was adamant she was singing the correct words.*

> *As a little boy Tom went to the Band of Hope and heartily sang, "My cup's full of Ronny Rover."*
>
> *In his reality, Ronny Rover was a swashbuckling, seafaring hero. Tom was very reluctant to accept the truth – that his cup was "full and running over".*

When they were older, Louise and Tom changed their reality and understood the generally perceived reality of their songs. However, even as little children we can change the reality we have created.

> *"When I was four or five, I was really frightened of the dark," said Maxine. "I used to demand that my mother left a night light on. Then one evening we had a power cut. I was really upset until my mother drew back the curtains in my bedroom. As I lay in bed, I could see the light from the stars and the moon. From then onwards I didn't need the light on when I was in bed. I realised at some level that I had created my own fear of night-time. I was really happy when I changed this fear into an understanding that night-time had its own light to keep me company. And I still prefer sleeping with the curtains open!"*

---

[10] In *Collins Dictionary of the English Language.*

In this way, Maxine changed her own reality. She was no longer afraid of night-time, but actually appreciated starlight and moonlight and has been able to derive pleasure from them ever since.

This reality-changing power is not possessed only by children. We each have this ability, even though we may not have recognised that we still use it.

> *Carol is an interior designer. She went to a social event where she met another designer to whom she happily chatted about work. Later on Carol learnt that this designer was very famous and successful.*
>
> *"If I had known that at the time," said Carol, "I would never have talked to her in such a relaxed way. I would have been in total awe of her."*

Carol had been safe in the first reality she had created; that this other designer was someone she could discuss design ideas with. By putting her on a pedestal, Carol changed this reality. When Carol discovered that the other designer was in a different business league from herself, she lost the confidence she had to talk to her naturally and with ease. In the previous reality she had this confidence.

By recognising that we have the ability to change our perception of reality we can create powerful changes for ourselves. A vivid example of this is contained in the following quotation from Anne Michaels' amazing novel *Fugitive Pieces*.[11]

Jakob, a Jewish boy aged about 10 years old, was rescued from the Holocaust by Athos and together they fled to Greece. Here, Athos hid Jakob from the Nazis in a small house for the duration of the war. Jakob explains how he coped.

> ***For four years I was confined to small rooms. But Athos gave me another realm to inhabit, big as the globe and expansive as time.***

[11] Taken from the book *Fugitive Pieces* by Anne Michaels published by Bloomsbury Publishing Plc in 1997.

> ***Because of Athos, I spent hours in other worlds then surfaced dripping, as from the sea. Because of Athos, our little house became a crow's nest, a Vinland peathouse. Inside the cave of my skull oceans swayed with monstrous ice-flows, navigated by skin-boats. Mariners hung from mizzenmasts and ropes made from walrus hides. Vikings rowed down the mighty rivers of Russia...***

Jakob created a reality for himself that transcended the confines of the small room and was as large as the world itself. What an amazing power this child had. What an amazing power we all have. **Reality does not remain fixed, as it appears to be. We can change it and indeed we do.**

Nine years ago I decided to have swimming lessons. Until then I had been unable to swim, except perhaps half a breadth of the local pool – and this with one foot on the bottom and with my head up. You see, I was unable to breathe under water. In fact, I would drown if I got my face wet. As for staying afloat. How could I possibly do that? I was sure to sink to the bottom. This was the reality I had created for myself.

Looking back, it seems odd that I could have believed this. After all, how was my body so different from that of other people who could swim happily with their heads under water and out of their depth as well? How could I have kidded myself that my reality was correct? Yet I had done so, and many family holidays spent watching everyone else enjoying themselves in the pool or sea were proof of that.

After a few lessons I began to realise that I could stay alive with my head under water. I could even take my feet off the bottom and remain afloat. Slowly I lost my fear of swimming. In fact I became obsessed with swimming for a while – going to the pool almost every day. Swimming became, and has remained, a source of great pleasure for me.

Perhaps I derive added satisfaction from the fact that I did this myself. I had a wonderfully patient teacher, I know, but somewhere along the way I changed my reality and overcame my fear of the water. When I did that I began to swim. I became a swimmer. I believed in my ability to swim. Swimming was a delight – not something to be frightened of.

I changed my reality from one where swimming was scary to one where swimming was a pleasure. I had exchanged fear of the water for love of the water. I had taught myself that I enjoy swimming. This was my new reality.

But this realisation was only half of the story. The other half was that I had originally created my own dread of swimming. If I accept that I had changed my reality from one of horror of swimming to one of love of swimming, I must also accept that I was the author of my original fear of swimming. The fact that I was afraid of the water came from within myself. I was physically capable of swimming, but somehow I had not allowed myself to swim. I had given my power away. By learning to swim I had not only changed my reality as far as being in water was concerned. I had also released the power I already had within me to conquer my own fears.

This understanding has amazing applications. If I can give up my fear of swimming I can also give up any fears I may have of people or other situations. As well as being the author of my own fear, I am also the dispeller of this fear.

Applying this thinking to harassment and bullying is very powerful. We can each change the reality as it appears to us. If we are afraid of someone else or intimidated by them, we need to recognise that at some level we have created this fear for ourselves. I am not saying we should blame ourselves or beat ourselves up about this. At the time our fear may well be a source of protection until we are ready or able to change.

But change we can. We can change our reaction to people and we can change the reality as we see it. We do not have to remain fearful or powerless. We can change how we look upon other people and different situations. We can do things differently. We can become **bully proof**.

The only person stopping me from changing my reality or my reaction to other people is myself and the only person stopping you from doing this is yourself.

Changing Your Reality!

Changing Your Reality!

Transcription of an exchange between the US Navy and the Canadian authorities, off the coast of Newfoundland.[12]

Americans *Please divert your course 15 degrees to the north to avoid a collision.*

Canadians *Suggest you divert your course 15 degrees to the south to avoid collision.*

Americans *This is the captain of a US Navy ship. I say again, divert your course.*

Canadians *No, I say again, you divert.*

Americans *This is the aircraft carrier USS Missouri. We are a very large warship of the US Navy. Divert your course now!*

Canadians *This is a lighthouse. Your call.*

[12] Quoted in *The Sunday Times*, 1st February 1998.

Exercise 3	**Whose reality?**
This exercise works well in small groups. First of all, answer the questions by yourself and then compare your answers with those of others in your group. Where you have a different answer from them, explain your perception and listen to theirs. Open your mind to understanding their reality. Can you begin to feel a change in yours?	
1. You find the smell of freshly brewed coffee irresistible.	Yes/No
2. You would be perfectly at ease with a live parrot on your shoulders.	Yes/No
3. Your idea of the ideal evening is spending it curled up in front of your favourite TV soap.	Yes/No
4. You would prefer to take an Arctic cruise rather than a Caribbean cruise?	Yes/No
5. You enjoy eating Marmite.	Yes/No
6. You prefer listening to heavy metal rather than opera.	Yes/No
7. You enjoy going to watch football matches.	Yes/No
8. Your ideal holiday would be camping in the Scottish Highlands.	Yes/No
9. Your favourite type of art is Post-Modernism.	Yes/No
10. You have always found mental arithmetic easy.	Yes/No

Exercise 4	**Letting in the moonlight**
List three work-related realities you would like to change. *e.g. I hate the team meetings which are long and unstructured.* 1. 2. 3.	
How would you like these realities to be? *e.g. I would like to think I have spent this time in a useful way.* 1. 2. 3.	
How can you change these realities yourself? *e.g. I could offer to chair the meetings myself or draw up the agenda, or, I could relax and enjoy being with other members of the team, even if the meetings are rather unproductive.* 1. 2. 3.	

Chapter 3

Staying on Course

Just as the American ship needed to change its reaction to avoid a collision, so we need to alter our reactions to harassers or bullies if we want to create a change in their behaviour.

A lighthouse had the power to change the course of a US Navy aircraft carrier and we, in our everyday lives, have the power to influence the behaviour of those around us.

Having used a naval analogy to make a point, it is worth dwelling a little longer in this area. According to newspaper reports, sexism, racism, anti-gay behaviour and bullying are rife in the army, air force and navy. Police forces and fire brigades, too, often have to defend themselves from claims of sexual and racial harassment. Outdated and prejudicial values in military and quasi military sectors of employment foster discriminatory behaviour against women, ethnic minorities and other people such as gays and lesbians, who do not fit the white, male, macho image.

Most of the few high-profile black soldiers in the Household Cavalry have left the regiment, citing the effects of long-term verbal abuse from their comrades in arms as the reason for their departure. Horror stories of bullying and harassment in the armed forces emerge from hearings and employment tribunals.

A male major in the army was disciplined for publicly stating that sexism, racism and class bias were widespread in the military. Senior officers joined his campaign for reform, claiming that in many aspects of military activity, women are at least as good as men and, in a number of areas, are considerably better. US research shows that women recruits are, on average, more intelligent than their male counterparts, score higher on personality tests, are not afraid of firing a gun and have a better record of accuracy when they do.

Yet, despite female prowess, at present only 7% of soldiers in the UK are women. This, together with the fact that only 1% are from ethnic minorities, confirms that racism and sexism have an endemic grip on the armed forces.

In spite of this background, every so often we hear about women who have broken through the military glass ceiling. A 33 year old beat male rivals to one of the key jobs on a Royal Navy warship as principal warfare officer. This post carries the responsibility for helping to direct offensive operations.

So, on the one hand, there are some women, albeit not many, who are successful in a male-dominated environment. They seem either impervious to the insidious effects of sexual harassment and bullying or to display such a confident image that sexual harassers or bullies know better than to take them on. Yet, on the other hand, there are people whose morale and sense of well being are severely undermined when they are subjected to abuse. To them it seems as if the odds are stacked against them to survive, let alone succeed.

It is an enigma that some women can cope and thrive in circumstances that severely affect others in a negative way. This quandary is encapsulated in a quotation from Helen Elaine Lee's novel, which describes the effect of bullying on Vesta, a young girl growing up in a city in northern USA around 1920.

> ***Though they, too, were all colored, her class mates made fun of Vesta's dark skin and she tried to make light of their jokes and toss their insults off, but once her tormentors discovered they had the power to get to her, she became the perfect target for abuse. She didn't understand why they had chosen her to pick on, and was puzzled by the fact that one of the instigators was a girl as dark as she was, who seemed to have convinced***

> ***herself otherwise. The exclusion overwhelmed her, made things tumble and swim, until she turned inward and settled it with the understanding that there was something about her that was different.***[13]

Vesta was clearly damaged by the abuse her classmates meted out to her. She seemed to lose all her power when she was subjected to their insults. Yet she did not know why she had been selected for the bullying as she was similar to the other girls as far as age and race were concerned.

We can find parallel cases to Vesta in the workplace. Some people cede their power to bullies and harassers. Some people are singled out for abuse. Yet the reverse is also true. Like the naval example cited above, some women do succeed in macho working environments.

- **Against all the odds some women cope successfully in sexist working environments.**
- **Some women seem to thrive and enjoy working in a macho culture that would cause many of us to feel harassed or bullied.**
- **There are women who stay on course, believing in themselves, despite the sexism and harassment they may be subjected to on a daily basis.**
- **And even more incredibly, some women create an aura that discourages or deflects sexism, bullying or harassment in the first place. In other words, they are bully proof.**

What are their secrets? What is different about these women that allows this to be so? What can we learn from them?

To find the answers to these questions I interviewed a range of women. They varied in age, occupation, ethnicity and background. However, they each had one thing in common. They successfully stayed on course, believing in their own

[13] Helen Elaine Lee, *The Serpent's Gift*, Scribner, New York, 1994.

worth, despite working in a macho environment that would deter many women.

The following case studies are representative of the sample. As you read them, see if you can determine:

- the similarities between the women despite the differences in their experiences
- the beliefs that allow them to remain true to themselves.

1. Carley – a CID officer

"After I had been in the police force for two years, I decided to try for the CID. I remember being told by all the male officers that I needed to get more experience and that I was not good enough for the CID. They constantly tried to undermine me by attempting to make me feel stupid when I went on calls.

"I remember thinking that I knew I was going to be a good CID officer and that I didn't care what the men said. I just felt the CID was right for me. I didn't ever let them get me down.

"I always knew I was as good if not better than most of them. I had this inner confidence. I had wanted to join the police since I was a young girl. My mother had been a great influence on me and always taught me to believe that if you wanted to be something in life, then no one will stop you. She didn't have any doubts about me when I joined the police force. And I was so tunnel visioned I didn't let other people's negative views upset me.

"I felt that being in the CID would be a whole new world that would be difficult. But I didn't see why I couldn't learn when I was in post. After all, no one was born knowing how to be a CID officer.

"The same happened a few years later when I asked to go to the Flying Squad. I spoke to my Detective Chief

Inspector who tried to put me off. He said the Flying Squad was a man's world and how did I think I could cope with people who were the equivalent of the Kray Twins. All I could think was, 'why not?' My Detective CI really tried to put me down, but I can remember sitting in his office one day and mentally squaring my shoulders as I thought, 'Who the hell are you to tell me I can't do a job when I know I can?' I knew I had never confronted burly armed robbers, but then I hadn't confronted drunken louts either before I joined the job. That was something you had to learn on the streets. You never know if you are going to be able to do police work until you get out there and do it!

"It never occurred to me that he was right. I knew I was right. I just thought he was a poor man who didn't understand how strong women really were!

"One day when I was in the CID, the river police found a body washed up at low tide. I was alone on duty with a young temporary detective who was learning the ropes. I took him with me to look at the body. I realised straightaway that there were suspicious circumstances so I set up a murder inquiry and in such cases the first police officer that sees the victim is with the body throughout the investigation. Eventually the senior officers came back from lunch and this same Detective CI began to delegate jobs. When I said that I had found the body, he said I couldn't be the forensic officer, it ought to be a man. So the young temporary detective was appointed the forensic officer. I protested loudly but he wouldn't change his mind.

"I knew I could have got upset and been really damaged by his attitude. But I also knew I had to salvage my self-esteem, which was constantly in danger of being battered by him. So I thought, 'It's his problem not mine. It's his loss that he can't see women doing responsible jobs in the force. If he's going to go through life like that, then he's missing out on a lot.'

"I knew I had the backing of other officers I worked with. Most of them came up to me and said I was more than capable of doing the job. So I didn't lose my self-confidence.

"I realised that as a police officer I didn't have to bully my way through life, be argumentative, nasty like some of the men. I never felt the need to be like the men - in fact I went out of my way to be feminine. I believed women had something different to offer from the men. I didn't have to become one of the boys - swilling pints of beer and swearing.

"I would go down the pub with them but I would leave when the party games started. My reputation was too important for me to lose it. If jokes went beyond a certain point I would give them one look and they'd know I was angry. It was really important to me that I kept my self-respect. I never forgot I was a woman. I knew I couldn't be exactly the same as a male officer but I knew I could be as competent as the best of them."

2. Rachel - a young army officer

"When I first joined, the men stood up every time a female officer came into the room. I immediately told the senior officers I didn't want the men to do this. I wanted to be treated like the others. I believe it is important to behave like the other soldiers and not to expect special treatment because you are a woman. I didn't mind a certain amount of bad language and banter, even though the senior officer told the men to stop it. I didn't want the men to feel I was stopping them from behaving the way they usually did.

"I never asked for preferential treatment and I think it was the women who wanted this who were resented. They called me nicknames, like they did the men. I thought this was all right, as I believed it was better to have nicknames to your face than behind your back. This meant you were accepted by the others and this led you to have a belief that you were OK.

"Men will treat you differently from the others if you are seen to need special privileges. Many army officers went to boarding school so they are not used to women. My older brothers and father prepared me for life with men. I know it is important to laugh and joke back with them.

"You have to be twice as good as the men to be accepted. They set higher standards for you. I have always been as fit and capable as they are and knowing I can do the job gives me great confidence. This in turn means you can deal with the men and cope with any sexism or bullying."

3. Teresa – a young army officer

"I was bullied by a commanding officer when I first joined one section. He said there were two things against me – that I was female and that I was in a non-combatant corps. So I thought to myself that I was going to show him that I could do the job as well as anyone else.

"I worked hard at being extra fit. I could do runs carrying weights as well as or even better than the men could. I believed it was important that he took me seriously and took all women in the army seriously. I had always believed that it doesn't get you anywhere shouting and bullying someone. It is better to talk to people, not bawl at them. I had a low opinion of this commanding officer as he shouted at me all the time. The lower my opinion of him became, the stronger I believed in myself. He was pathetic. He was universally disliked and it was not just me he was bullying.

"I also knew that I was brighter than he was. I knew my training and communication skills were excellent - much better than his. By speaking back to him, I was true to myself. The more I spoke up for myself, the more his bad attitude towards me reduced.

"A visiting brigadier made a sexist comment about me in front of my male colleagues at a social event. I said something back to him - funny but cutting. I felt OK about doing this - I think you should always make sure you say something back to people who are sexist.

"Deep down I believe I am better than my male officer. I say to myself he is not worth the effort, sod him. I know I am capable of doing my job well. I've seen life - I'm streetwise not just Sandhurst. These men don't know what the real world is like. They are blinkered. I'm not going to be bothered by their sexism. I'm ambitious and am going to do well. They won't stop me.

"My self-esteem was low when I left Sandhurst because I was injured. It took me a good year to build myself up physically. So during this period I was more fragile if someone shouted at me. When I got back into sport I was happier with myself. When I was fitter I was more confident, so I could deal with it better. I believe and know I can do as well as the guys."

4. Kindy - a young black engineer

"There are three women in our team and the rest are men. The men put up some girlie calendars that we found offensive. I was the only woman prepared to speak up about this. I went to the boss and when I said we felt degraded by the calendars he just laughed. So I looked at him sternly and he quickly changed his expression. He asked if I would mind if they put the calendars in a corner of the room where they wouldn't be so prominent but I said that I did. So he agreed to tell the men to take them down.

"All the men knew it was me who had complained about the posters, but I didn't care. I felt clear and confident about speaking my mind. I knew the other women agreed with my point of view and were glad I had done something about it. I believed it was important to let the men know that women work here too and their feelings have to be considered.

"I believe in making sure people understand what I believe in. They might not agree with my views but that doesn't matter. I find it easier to challenge sexism when I know the other women feel the same and I am helping them too. I feel good when I challenge what I find unacceptable. I feel much better by challenging than by letting something pass."

5. Sarah - an executive

"If someone wants to put me in the position where I'm the little woman, quite frankly it reflects badly on them - not me - they are the one with the problem. I'm not going to take someone else's rubbish on board.

"I accept what people say until it gets to the stage where it starts to encroach on the things that are really important to me. Then the barriers come down and I withdraw. If I think people aren't going to respect the trust I put in them, why should I abuse myself?

"Being honest and open is important, as is listening to what the other person has to say. But I expect respect in return - it is a mutual thing, not one way. I am capable of resolve. I do not let people manipulate me or push me around. I have an inner strength, not in the sense of controlling somebody else, but of being sure about who I am. And if they don't like it that's their problem.

"If I demonstrate what I think is right, that is as much as I can do. I can't make them do anything. I believe it's OK to be me. I'll go a long way to meet the other person's point of view, but if they don't understand me, well that's OK too."

6. Aileen - a senior director

"I am the only female board member and the youngest too. I use my instincts to guide me through. I stick to my principles - if I don't know enough about something, then I tend to back off until I have more information or my instincts are firmed out. I believe I am the only fresh blood here. Things were not good when I first came, so I knew they could only get better. This made me feel secure about trying my ideas.

"I am a quick thinker and have a vision for the company. I am quick to speak out and have a reputation for saying what I think. I am frank and won't let meetings go off course. I believe in keeping the board on track when people go off at a tangent.

"When the profits grow, I know I am right. If I believe in something then I fervently follow it. I am guided by my gut feelings and instincts and I know when something is right. I've never needed reassurance from other people. I have always had to fight for what I believed. If I get another person's reassurance that is a perk.

"I am determined and committed as well as enthusiastic. My team is enthusiastic too. They like having fun but they work hard. I believe this is the response I get because I give out those signals.

"I am a strong leader because I am a believer. I am prepared to stand out in front even if no one is supporting me. I am a doer and this makes people deliver. When they see I am convinced about something they are prepared to follow me. I believe every problem is solvable. If I said I wasn't sure they wouldn't have any faith in me.

"I try very hard to allow people to challenge me. I know I am a strong and blunt person and some people struggle with confronting me. I encourage people to question me and make me justify my ideas. I know I am a good communicator. Yet I dismiss this as a strength because I don't find it difficult. A strength to me is something I find hard to do and have had to learn. Communication has always come easy to me. Yet I know others who find it difficult. I think it is a very female quality. Men say I have taught them the benefits of communication. Yet I know my female friends are really good at it.

"Male culture doesn't encourage openness. Men need to keep things private in case their mistakes are known. I think it would help in the boardroom if men could communicate better. They are more concerned about losing face and status. All this doesn't mean I am soft. When someone has done something wrong one glare from me and they know about it."

7. Laura – a student

"I've always had many boys for friends and always found it easy to mix with them on an equal footing. I've never felt undermined or harassed by them. Yet often the boys seem to give my girl friends a hard time.

"When we are down the pub having a friendly argument some of the girls get very upset by the boys' attitude. I enjoy arguing - having a heated discussion. One evening we were talking about whether girls should play football professionally. I found I could put across my argument in a way that was heard by the boys. Yet the boys were dismissive towards the other girls present.

"Although I was getting really agitated and frustrated that the boys wouldn't accept that girls should play football professionally, I didn't let them see how I was feeling. I concentrated on giving a good logical argument and I became more forceful and powerful as I went on. I think it is important when talking to blokes not to get too emotional if you want your point of view to be heard.

"To me it is important to communicate effectively and to put my theories over. I know my argument is worth listening to and is as good if not better than that of the boys. I believe other people are as interested in what I am saying as they are in what they are saying. I even feel a little superior because I think my opinions are right. Yet I accept it is as important to listen to their point of view as it is to express my own."

Different women, different points of view – yet similar outcomes. An ability to remain on course, believing in themselves, despite the odds.

The Caravan[14]

The desert was all sand in some stretches, and rocky in others. When the caravan was blocked by a boulder, it had to go around it; if there was a large rocky area, they had to make a major detour. If the sand was too fine for the animals' hooves, they sought a way where the sand was more substantial. In some places, the ground was covered with the salt of dried-up lakes. The animals balked at such places, and the camel drivers were forced to dismount and unburden their charges. The drivers carried the freight themselves over such treacherous footing, and then reloaded the camels. If a guide were to fall ill or die, the camel drivers would draw lots and appoint a new one.

"But all this happened for one basic reason: no matter how many detours and adjustments it made, the caravan moved toward the same compass point. Once obstacles were overcome, it returned to its course, sighting on a star that indicated the location of the oasis. When the people saw that star shining in the morning sky, they knew they were on the right course toward water, palm trees, shelter, and other people.

[14] Paulo Coelho, *The Alchemist*, Thorsons, an imprint of Harper Collins Publishers Ltd, London, 1995.

Exercise 5	**Staying on course**
Identify two people you know who always seem to you to stay on course, believing in themselves, despite opposition from others.	**Ask them to think about a time when they felt really sure of themselves. Ask them to imagine that this is happening now. As they do so, ask them to describe it to you as if it were happening now by using the present tense.** **As they are associating into this situation, ask them what they are believing about themselves as they remain strong.**
1.	
2.	

Exercise 6	**Believing in yourself**
Think about a time when you really believed in yourself – your capabilities and power. It can be at any time in your life and doesn't have to be related to work.	**Fully associate into this occasion as if it is happening now. See, hear and feel what it is like.** **As you are associating into the occasion as if it is happening now, list what you are believing as you relive the situation.** *e.g. no one can stop me from doing this* or *I have a right to be listened to.*

Chapter 4

Charting Your Own Course

The women featured in the case studies in Chapter 3 stay on course, believing in themselves, despite the odds stacked against them. Even when they are bullied or harassed by a more senior member of staff, or intimidated by male colleagues or friends, they remain determined to stay true to themselves.

All these women have one thing in common. They made a choice, consciously or subconsciously, not only to cope but to be successful in macho environments. The key word here is **choice**. Never did they doubt that this choice was available to them. Never did they fail to exercise it.

Carley explained this when she talked about the attitude of her DCI. She said she could have been damaged by his attitude but knew she had to salvage her self-esteem, so she chose to believe that it was his problem and his loss, not hers. Teresa was bullied by a commanding officer but this did not deter her. Instead she chose to prove to him that she could do the job as well as anyone else.

The remarkable power of choosing to remain on course, believing in yourself, was summarised by Brian Keenan when talking about his four-and-a-half-year captivity in Beirut.[15] Even during his darkest hour, Brian believed:

> ***The essential choice you have is you can choose to be like a wounded dog in your mind, or you can run before***

[15] The author was fortunate enough to attend a talk by Brian Keenan in Henley, England in 1997. For details of his remarkable story, see Brian Keenan, *An Evil Cradling*, Vintage, London, 1992.

it and be your own pied piper. Even though it requires a huge amount of courage to be unafraid of the consequences, you can take control.

Brian chose to 'be his own pied piper' charting his own course. He did not allow his captors to destroy his belief in himself and his determination to come out of that terrible situation with his personal dignity in tact. He not only remained true to what he believed – he deliberately chose to do so.

As well as **choice**, the other important factor here is **belief**. To paraphrase Henry Ford, whether you think you can, or whether you think you can't, you are probably right.

The case studies in Chapter 3 exemplify this point, so let's look a little more closely at what the women believe and how their beliefs influence their situations.

❖ The power of belief

Despite the differences in the ages, lives and details of the experiences of these seven women, there are many similarities in the beliefs they hold.

Although they did not use the same words, all of them in some way echoed Sarah's belief – **It's OK to be me**. This belief is founded in a strongly held perception that, despite what their male colleagues or bosses say about them or how they behave towards them, they are fundamentally superior to, or at least as good as, the men.

Although several inferred that to succeed in a macho workplace a woman needs to be twice as good as a man, these women are not daunted by this. They know that, like the men, they were not born knowing how to do their jobs. However, they are determined to work hard, develop their skills and be even more successful than the men. As Teresa said, "I believe and know I can do as well as the guys."

Carrying this strong belief helps the women deal with sexist knocks and abuse. Carley believed she was going to be a good CID officer and if you want to achieve something in life, nothing and no one can stop you. With this came a belief that you can choose to challenge sexism and not allow it to damage or humiliate you. Laura believes that other people are interested in her point of view. What is important is that they listen to her. She is sure that her opinion counts, so it does not necessarily matter if the boys agree with her or not. She knows her opinions are valid and this is all that is important to her.

By believing **It's OK to be me**, all the women in the case studies know that if men are sexist or abusive it reflects badly on them, not on the women themselves.

❖ What has to be true for the women to believe in themselves

All the women hinted at certain criteria that have to be in place for them to continue to stay on course, believing in themselves.

When Kindy is sure that the other women feel as she does and that she is helping them too, she finds it easier to challenge sexism. It is important to her to know that she is helping others as well as helping herself.

For Sarah, honesty is fundamental to her way of being. If she knows she has been honest and open she demands these qualities from those around her. She expects respect in return for the respect she gives to others. If at any time she thinks she is being treated in a disrespectful way, she feels free to challenge or discount the views of others.

Aileen is determined, committed and enthusiastic in her approach to her work and she expects these same characteristics from her team. She believes no one has the right to undermine her as long as she has demonstrated her commitment and determination.

Rachel and Teresa work hard at keeping fit to ensure their skills are on a par or superior to those of the men. They are determined to make sure the men do not have an excuse for belittling or undermining them. Being on top form gives them the confidence to continue believing in themselves.

❖ How do the women know they are OK?

As we read the case studies we are confident that the women know they are OK. How, though, do they know this? Where does this confidence come from? Who gives it to them?

The answer to these questions lies very much within the women themselves. They know they are OK because they tell themselves they are. They do not need to check with other people that it is OK for them to take a certain stance. They do not have to ask anyone else for reassurance. They check within themselves that it is OK and they accept their own opinions and encouragement. They do not rely on others for this support.

Several state they are happy when their approach is beneficial to other women or colleagues. In some ways they see themselves as an advocate for others. However, it is with inner determination that they chart their own course, confident they themselves know that what they are doing is right for them.

How to achieve this level of self belief is an issue we will look at later in this chapter.

❖ Male and female styles

The case studies give us a snapshot of women who are successfully working in predominantly male environments. It is not surprising, therefore, that they allude to the differences and similarities of male and female styles of behaviour and working patterns. The women make some interesting points relating to men and women working together which contribute to their success in male-dominated worlds.

Carley realised that men are not born knowing how to be good police officers any more than women are. This knowledge gave her the confidence to learn on the job and not feel deterred by her DCI's sexist remarks about her abilities. She accepted that she could not be exactly the same as a male officer but, on the other hand, she knew she could be as competent as the best of them.

Rachel believes it is important that she is treated in the same way as the male army officers. She does not want any preferential treatment because she is a woman. This, she feels, would cause resentment from the men and would stop them from accepting her as one of the team.

Aileen is determined that she will not appear soft in front of her male directors. She is keen to encourage open communication and believes that women in general recognise the benefits of good communication. However, she matches the male style by being tough when she needs to be in order to retain her strong position in front of her male colleagues.

Laura recognises that it is important to liken her discursive style to the male style of argument, which she refers to as logical and forceful. She believes some of her girl friends are dismissed in a sexist way because they become emotional when challenged by the boys. Laura says that the boys talk over the girls' points of view when they notice the girls are becoming emotional.

So, to a certain extent, the women realise that matching the male style is vital if they are to be accepted in macho workplaces. They are keen to be treated as equal to the men and in order to achieve this they recognise they should liken their approach to the male way of doing things. They do not expect special treatment that would set them apart from the men.

What is clear from these women is that this ability to find a corresponding style to the male style does not cause them to betray or abandon their own feminine characteristics. At no time do they adopt the characteristics of the male style that they find offensive. They have a fundamental belief in the contribution women and a female style can make.

Carley exemplified this when she said that she had no intention of using the argumentative and bullying approach of some of her male colleagues. She went out of her way to be feminine and felt she didn't have to become one of the boys, swilling pints of beer and swearing down the pub. She felt that a female approach to policing has a very important part to play.

She would go to the pub with the men but she placed clear parameters around the behaviour she was prepared to accept. She realised how important it was to keep her good reputation and she would leave the pub when the male behaviour crossed a certain line.

When Kindy found the behaviour of the men in the office offensive, she was quick to make a stand, even though she was the only woman prepared to do this. Aileen values her female style of communication and encourages people to question her. This, she knows, is different from the male approach, which she defines as being more concerned with losing face and status. She realises she has a contribution to make by introducing her more female style to the boardroom.

On the one hand, these women are successful because they **liken** their approach to the male approach – they match some of their behaviour to that of the male. However, on the other, they never forget the value of the French expression *vive la différence*. They do not apologise for being women and do not allow their female qualities to be undermined or discounted when working in male environments.

❖ A powerful representation of themselves

When I was talking to the women, several of them used metaphorical language to describe themselves as they stayed on course, believing in themselves. Examples of these are as follows:

- **"I'm a lion – strong and powerful. Unlike him – he's weak."**
- **"I picture myself as a butterfly which can open its wings and fly away. This is not in the sense of escaping but of positively going towards freedom."**
- **"I've been likened to an exocet missile – I can't be deflected and I go at 100 miles an hour."**

- **"I'm a cat, not too dominant or overbearing, but able to calm things down."**

Although these metaphors vary, they nevertheless have common characteristics.

They each represent a powerful image, with the missile and the lion as obvious examples. The butterfly, however fragile, has the ability to plot its own course and the cat, while independent and autonomous, understands how to get its own way.

The metaphorical representations described by the women suggest movement, dynamism and impact. All these creatures live independently from human control. Even domestic cats do things in their own way, as any cat owner will tell you. And exocet missiles, once they are released, take on a life of their own.

So what about the rest of us?

The women chosen for the case studies are successfully coping with living or working in macho environments. They were selected not because they had hit the headlines or broken the glass ceiling. They were picked as being representative of women flourishing in male-dominated environments that have reputations for being anti-female and sexist. They feel good about themselves despite attempts by others to demean or belittle them. They are resourceful despite harassment and bullying. And they have developed personas that either deflect sexism or discourage it from occurring in the first place.

"But," you are saying, "what about me? I'm not the same as these women. My situation is different."

We are, of course, all unique and our circumstances vary considerably. We behave in different ways and receive different treatment from other people. We live and work in a variety of environments and have a range of skills and capabilities. None of our experiences are exactly the same, nor indeed are our histories and futures.

Yet, I believe that by reflecting on these case studies we can learn a great deal. They offer us valuable lessons that will make a real difference in our lives.

And we don't have to be women to learn from the studies. Men, too, will benefit from considering how these women succeed in staying on course, believing in themselves. I deliberately chose women working in macho environments, such as the army or the police force, as I wanted to illustrate success in very testing workplaces. I believe if these women have the power to cope, each of us can find that power if we choose to do so – woman or man.

We will learn to do this by considering

- what these women believe
- how they set criteria to be fulfilled
- and the strategies for staying on course they then adopt.

In other words, we can use these women as models.

1. Take on an empowering belief

We each of us carry beliefs that may have been a part of us for a very long time. Often we have held them since our childhood when influential figures, such as parents or teachers, told us:

> "You're a sissy if you cry."
>
> "Girls can't play football."
>
> "This is no place for a woman."
>
> "You are a hopeless speller."

Over the years these beliefs become a part of who we are. They influence our behaviour, they determine what decisions we make and they even limit the options we choose for ourselves. Remember how I believed I was too frightened to swim? Think about the wonderful seaside holiday opportunities I denied myself as a result.

But all is not lost. **We can change our beliefs** – as indeed I did in relation to swimming. Or, at the very least, we can try new beliefs for size and presuppose they are true.

To help us take on a new and empowering belief, let's consider the beliefs of the women in the case studies. They can be summarised as follows:

✓ **It's OK to be me.** (Perhaps the most fundamental belief of the women selected.)

✓ **I believe in myself even if others don't.**

✓ **I know I am good at what I do.**

✓ **I believe others are just as interested in my point of view as they are in their own.**

✓ **I have the right to say what I think.**

✓ **I know when something is right for me.**

As you read this list you will recognise the one that immediately makes sense to you – the one that you know will make such a difference to your life.

Spend a few moments considering how empowering it will be when you truly hold this belief in all that you do. Even if you can't yet accept this belief one hundred per cent, pretend that you can.

Run through a scenario that will take place in the next day or two, perhaps something that you have been dreading or putting off tackling. As you think about it, take on this empowering belief and sense how pleasant and liberating it feels. Think through what you will see, hear and feel as you enact this situation. Imagine the reactions of your friends or colleagues and how they will recognise you as a strong and powerful person.

When you throw off your limiting beliefs, you will in turn discard the limiting behaviour that has been holding you back from coping in a bullying or harassing environment. By taking on the empowering belief that **It is OK to be you**, you will act and behave in a resourceful and determined way.

And for those of you who are saying, "Well, that's all right for you, but at present I can't yet relate these beliefs to myself," I say **pretend that you can – presuppose that you do hold these beliefs**.

The mind is a funny thing. Unconsciously it does not distinguish between what is real and what is imagined. If you tell yourself that you believe in something, your mind will accept it.

Go on, have a go and see what a difference it makes!

To help you even further, refer back to Exercise 6 at the end of the previous chapter. In that exercise you were asked to think about a time when you really believed in yourself – your capabilities and power. If you haven't yet done it, spend a few moments now thinking about it.

Fully associate with that moment. See, hear and feel what it was like. As you are associating into that occasion, list the beliefs you are carrying. How similar are they to those held by the women in the case studies? Very similar I am sure.

As well as modelling these women, you have the chance to model yourself! **You have been successful many times in your life**. Think about the beliefs you held when you were. Notice how similar they were each time you were successful and how close they are to the beliefs detailed in our case studies.

You already have the strategy to be successful. Use it! Remind yourself of these beliefs each time something daunting and forbidding happens to you. Experience the power these beliefs give you!

2. Understand your core values

The women I interviewed were acutely aware of the values they held. If certain of these values were not met, they felt that they had a right to take action. For example, Sarah said RESPECT is very important to her. If she is not treated with respect, she knows she has a right to object to someone's behaviour or withdraw from a situation. The knowledge that her criterion of respect has to be fulfilled gives her the benchmark with which to judge other people and her relationships with them. When this value is not met, she knows she does not have to put up with the way she is being treated.

We each of us have core values or criteria that are fundamental to the way in which we live and relate to other people. Being aware of these values can help considerably when we are faced with situations we find uncomfortable.

Let's consider further the criterion of RESPECT. If we are harassed or bullied we are not treated with respect. We may feel belittled, humiliated, frightened or indeed a combination of these negative emotions. We may feel our dignity has been damaged and that we are operating in stressful conditions.

Understanding that RESPECT is one of our core values and that the harassment or bullying contravenes the criteria we set for ourselves gives us permission to challenge unacceptable behaviour. As we recognise that one of our criteria is not being met, we feel empowered to object to what is happening to us, either by confronting the behaviour or withdrawing from the situation, or at least by seeking support from others.

By establishing what our core values are, we can set limits for what we are prepared to endure and liberate ourselves from being reluctant or unsure about speaking out for ourselves. If our core values are being violated, we as human beings are being violated and that is unacceptable.

As you go through Exercise 7 at the end of this chapter, you will determine the core values that make your life meaningful and worthwhile.

When you know your core values, you will know what choices you wish to make when confronted with unacceptable behaviour.

3. Check out what is right for you

The women in the case studies have the following in common:

- They are clear how they feel about the situations they face.
- They know what is right for them.
- They are certain of their strengths and capabilities.
- They are aware of the boundaries they place around themselves.
- They know how they react to certain behaviour.

Occasionally they are pleased to learn that when they challenge harassment they are also helping other people in their workplaces or supporting their friends. However, they do not have to check out with others what is right for them. They check this out with themselves.

Remember your answers to Exercise 6 when you identified times in your life when you believed in yourself and were powerful and successful. The fact that you selected these occasions is evidence that you know when you are on course and sure that what you are doing and believing is OK for you. You already do this in a variety of situations. You already check out what is right for you. You have a strategy for doing this.

I invite you, therefore, to transfer this strategy over to areas of your life you would like to change. Remind yourself that **It is OK to be you**, that it's OK to feel the way you do and to wish to challenge unacceptable behaviour. You do not need to ask someone else's permission to feel like this. You can reassure yourself that you know when something is right for you and that you have a right to say what you think.

You already use this strategy successfully. As you use it when you are faced with unacceptable behaviour, you will experience a sense of making powerful choices.

4. Match the other person

Laura recognises that the boys she knows are more likely to accept arguments if they are presented in a logical and forceful way. She finds that if she adopts this style the boys are likely to listen to her and not dismiss her point of view out of hand. Rachel recognises that it is important for her to behave in a similar style to the men if she wants to be accepted by them. This involves putting up with their nicknames and joining in some of the joking and laughter.

Thus the women match their style to that of the men and they find this is paramount to building a reasonable working relationship with them.

This does not mean that the women either allow their own standards to fall or they condone unacceptable behaviour. Remember how Carley left the pub when things began to get out of hand.

What it does mean is that accommodating the different approaches other people have can be key to developing an acceptable way of operating with them. But it is vital to remember what boundaries you have set and to stick to them. If people begin to transgress these boundaries, you have a right to say so.

Think about a situation you would like to improve – perhaps one where you find another person's behaviour or attitude problematic. What can you do differently to try to build rapport with this person? In what way can you match their style of working?

I am not proposing that you should adopt a style of behaviour incongruent with your core values. What I am suggesting is that you modify your way of working in a way that matches the other person. Remember what we discussed in Chapter 2:

> ***You cannot change another person, but you can change your reactions to them.***

Let me give you an example of when this was done successfully.

> *Phil felt bullied by his co-workers and his boss. Whenever he tried to explain a problem he had with his working conditions, he felt they never gave him enough time to explain the situation in a way that he found satisfactory. They were impatient with him, used coarse language and often walked away before he had finished.*
>
> *He started to analyse how they interacted with each other. He noticed they spoke in quite a quick and abrupt style. They did not have long friendly conversations, nor did they dwell on a topic for too long. The boss always seemed under pressure and issued short notes if he wanted changes in the staff's working methods.*
>
> *Phil began to match his colleagues' style of talking. He thought in advance what he wanted to say when he had a problem to discuss, and explained his concerns in as few sentences as possible. He made sure he came to the point very quickly and spoke in a direct, confident style. Then he returned to his work and let them get on with theirs. He began writing short memos to his boss if he wanted to put forward his point of view.*
>
> *After a while he noticed a difference in their attitude. They began to listen to him and involve him in their brief and work-related conversations. The boss seemed to take on board his concerns.*
>
> *At no time, however, did Phil resort to the coarse language of the other staff. He believed he could communicate without swearing or abuse. But by matching most of his colleagues' style of communication, he began to feel there were some improvements in his relationship with them.*

5. Take on a powerful representation of yourself

Remember how some of the women in the case studies had a powerful metaphorical image of themselves. These metaphors were representations of the power and resourcefulness they wished to portray.

Think about yourself in the powerful states you listed in Exercise 6 when you believed in yourself and stayed on course.

- What would be a representation of you at times like that?
- Who are you when you are strong and powerful?
- Are you an animal or a bird?
- If you draw a picture of a determined you charting your own course, what would it look like?

This metaphor of yourself is yours and yours alone. At times when you feel undermined or challenged, take on the feelings of your metaphor, picture yourself in this way, talk to yourself as if you were this creature or object. Practise it now and enjoy the experience. If you were Carley, you would be roaring like a lion. Think how powerful that would be!

Above are the five components that make up *a strategy* you already possess for being resourceful and determined.

1. **Take on an empowering belief**
2. **Understand your core values**
3. **Check out what is right for you**
4. **Match the other person**
5. **Take on a powerful representation of yourself**

Use this strategy as you chart your own course through life. By so doing, when you feel you are being bullied or harassed you will become powerful like the women in the case studies. You will begin to behave in a way that demands respect and dignity. You will be seen as a force to be reckoned with – not a victim to be demeaned or belittled.

Let's look at this strategy being used by someone who was in a bullying situation.

Hazel had been working for a small company as a secretary for two months. During that time she had received little training or induction into her job.

Her boss, Steve, never explained how he wanted Hazel to do his work, but was very critical when the work was not up to the standard he set. He gave Hazel instructions in a very patronising way and expected her to run errands and be at his beck and call.

Hazel never took a lunch break and rarely finished her work in time to go home at 5.30pm. She wasn't paid overtime, nor was she given any thanks for the hard work she put in to the job. She only ever received criticisms and put-downs. She felt she had no control over her working day and that her working life was being dictated by Steve. She said she felt he treated her as if she was a child and consequently she feared she had begun acting like one when he was around.

1. Take on an empowering belief

I asked Hazel to think of a time in the past when she had been completely in control, a time when she believed in her capabilities and was choosing the direction in which she wanted to go.

She gave me two examples.

- The first was when she goes horse riding, her greatest love.
- The second was when she bought her new house. She went on her own to view it and decided by herself that she and her husband would buy it – without his seeing it.

I asked her to fully associate into these times and to describe what she could see, hear and feel at those moments. I then asked her what she believed about herself and her capabilities.

She said she believed:

- She was in control.
- She was a grown up in charge of the situation.
- She was directing the operation.

By going through this process, Hazel realised for herself that at times in her life she was a very powerful person.

2. Understand your core values

I went through an exercise with Hazel in which she began to clarify her core values. To help her do this, I asked her to think about times when she was riding and when she chose the new house and to focus on what was important for her at that time. She came up with the following list:

- Freedom to choose
- Challenge
- Security

3. Check out what is right for you

Hazel said that when she was at work she had lost her confidence to make decisions and take control of her workload. She had begun to rely on Steve telling her what to do and when to do it. Even if she believed she had done a good job, she was easily persuaded by Steve that she should do her work more quickly or give priority to what he said was urgent. She knew this was causing her stress, as she was not able to prioritise her work in a way that was effective for her.

When she was riding, however, she did not have to check with anyone else that she was riding well. She knew she was doing OK. She knew when the horse was at ease. She was secure in her abilities and felt free to choose what to do.

When she chose the new house, she was immediately sure that this was the right house. She did not have to check it out with her husband.

4. Match the other person

Hazel explained that Steve was abrupt in his manner towards her. He was constantly in a hurry, never took into account the pressure she was under, and never had time for small talk. He just issued orders and became very impatient with her when she did not understand a new procedure or something that hadn't been explained to her.

When she began to analyse Steve's style, Hazel realised it was very different from her own. She had always tried to be accommodating and pleasant towards Steve and to ask him for clarification to make sure she understood the way he wanted her to do a task.

5. Take on a powerful representation of yourself

Hazel thought of a metaphor for herself when she was successfully on course, believing in her worth and ability, for example when she made a decision about the new house. She likened herself to a whirlwind. On the outside there was activity and movement, but inside there was power and peace.

6. Putting it all together

By going through the above components, Hazel began to realise she already had a strategy for staying on course, believing in herself.

She knew that her present way of working was not meeting her core values of security and freedom to choose. By taking on her own empowering belief that she was a grown up in charge of the situation, she altered her approach to her job. She began to say no to Steve when he overloaded her with work. She worked at the pace that suited her – quickly and efficiently – and she started to go out of the office at lunchtime each day. She decided when and if she was willing to work late and if she wasn't she pointedly walked out of the office at 5.30pm.

She reminded herself that she knew when she had done a good job and refused to allow Steve to undermine her with his criticisms. She said to herself that it was his problem if he doesn't like me and my way of dealing with clients. She knew she was not being rude to them and that was enough for her.

She stopped trying to engage Steve in conversations and quietly worked as quickly as possible. She never went to him with problems. If there was something she did not understand she would ask one of the other people in the office so as not to give him the chance to be critical, angry or impatient with her.

She began to think of herself as a powerful whirlwind that despite the activity and hard work was remaining calm inside. She even devised a rather disparaging metaphor for Steve that helped her think differently towards him when he was being unpleasant. But perhaps I had better not say any more about that!

By using this strategy, Hazel began to feel more resourceful and sure of herself, despite the unpleasantness she faced at work. Slowly, Steve began to treat her with more respect. He realised she was not going to allow him to push her around. He actually seemed relieved when she arrived for work one morning after his unpleasantness had caused her to walk out the previous evening.

"I don't try to please Steve now," she said, "because I know I can't. I no longer need his reassurance because I know I've done a good job."

In this way, Hazel became more in control of her working life and less at the mercy of her boss. In other words, she became **bully proof**.

Exercise 7	**Determining your values**
A. List below three people and three activities in your life that are very important to you. *e.g. going on holiday each year.*	**By the side of each person and activity named, write down what is important to you about the person or activity.** *e.g. I get love and security from X.* *e.g. I get fun/freedom/relaxation from my holiday.*
People	
1.	1.
2.	2.
3.	3.
Activities	
1.	1.
2.	2.
3.	3.
B. Look at the list of values that you have listed in the column under A. Words such as peace, freedom, etc. **Go through the list and underline the words that appear more than once and/or the ones which you believe are the most important to you.** **Write these words on the right.**	

C. Looking at the list in B above, try to rank the values in order of priority. Say to yourself, "If I could keep only one of these values for the rest of my life, which one would it be? If I had to give them up, which one would I hold on to until the last possible moment?" **Write these values on the right in the order of priority.**	1. 2. 3. 4.

Keep this list and look at it occasionally. Refine and revise it if and when you wish. You may not need to. Remind yourself frequently of your core values. They are yours and no one can take them away from you.

Chapter 5

The Ripple Effect

> ***My mother stands behind my father and his head leans against her. As he eats, she strokes his hair. Like a miraculous circuit, each draws strength from the other.***
>
> ***I see that I must give what I most need.***[16]

We are not islands. We are each a part of a system. Our systems include our nearest friends and relations, our work colleagues, our neighbours, the rest of our community and many more people. Our behaviour affects those around us, just as their behaviour affects us. When we are sad, our sadness impacts on others. When we are happy, our happiness creates happiness in others. Like a pebble in a pond, a little change in our behaviour is a ripple spreading out of our control.

> *A young mum was walking down the high street, hand in hand with her toddler. The little boy asked his mum for something and she replied in an abrupt manner. Her son was upset by this and began to cry. The mum became angry and shouted at the child, who in turn started to wail.*

I am not criticising the mum. We all get tired and frustrated at times with young children and what can seem like their incessant demands. But the mum and child are an example of how a little pebble can cause big ripples. A chance remark by the child caused irritation in the mum that, in turn, led to a few moments of misery between the two of them. They were each part of a miraculous circuit – impacting upon each other and receiving what they were giving out.

---

[16] Taken from the book *Fugitive Pieces* by Anne Michaels published by Bloomsbury Publishing Plc in 1997.

A little later on the mum realised that things were getting out of hand and gave the child a big cuddle and wiped his tears. In a flash, she had used her influence to make things better between them. After receiving the comfort he needed, the child in turn gave his mum the smiles that helped her cope with her tiredness and frustration. The behaviour of one affected the behaviour of the other. The ripple continued.

If each of us is part of a system, it follows that we are all a part of the bullying and harassing circuit. Just as a mother and child can trigger the other's behaviour and emotions, we each play a role in creating workplace atmospheres and relationships. We cannot stop the ripple effect of our behaviour and attitudes, we can only add to it.

This is not to say that we are to blame for the unpleasant behaviour of bullies and harassers. I am saying, however, that we are part of the system that they operate in. Just as we are not islands, they are not islands either.

It may help us to cope with unacceptable behaviour at work if we consider for a moment how this ripple effect operates in the workplace.

> *"We had all been looking forward to our new manager coming," Mary told me, "but somehow she and I got off on the wrong foot. She seemed to want to destroy me from the start. She pulled to bits in front of people everything I had done. She started asking junior staff to redo my work, implying that I wasn't capable of doing it correctly. This was really demeaning.*
>
> *"Instead of standing up for myself, I kept apologising for everything I did. I used to feel sick when I heard her coming into the office.*
>
> *"In meetings she would always slam down my ideas. But I never accepted her ideas either. The junior staff said I looked sullen when I was at a meeting with my manager. There was this no-go zone between us."*

From what Mary said, her manager usurped her power and belittled and bullied her. This caused Mary to lose her confidence and feel under considerable stress.

However, Mary admitted she appeared sulky in meetings and did not agree with the manager's ideas. Both Mary and the manager were a part of the same system. The behaviour of one of them led to a reaction in the other.

This tit-for-tat game exacerbated the poor relationship between the two of them until it was difficult to be certain who was giving out this behaviour and who was receiving it.

> *Jenny is a young graduate employed in a responsible position in a local authority. She is bright and confident and very capable of doing her job. She was having an unhappy time with her manager, Elaine, an older woman who had been running the department for many years.*
>
> *According to Jenny, Elaine looked upon the department as her family. She had no children of her own and was very motherly towards her flock. However, this motherliness turned into anger if she felt that Jenny was not doing her work exactly how she, Elaine, wanted her to. Yet Jenny felt that Elaine never really explained to her what she should do and wouldn't trust Jenny just to get on with the job.*
>
> *As we worked through the issues together, Jenny began to realise that Elaine was acting like a domineering parent who wouldn't listen to her point of view and always knew best. But after a while, Jenny recognised that she was playing a part in this scenario. When she and Elaine had a tête-à-tête to try to resolve the problems between them, Jenny admitted she would never look Elaine in the eye. She muttered her reluctant agreement to whatever Elaine said and, sulkily and begrudgingly, accepted Elaine's authority over her.*

Just as Jenny resented Elaine playing the role of unreasonable parent, Elaine probably felt unhappy that she had a defiant 'teenager' in her 'family' to deal with. In this instance, the circuit they had created was destructive to both of them. The ripples of their behaviour affected them both.

> ***"There's nothing I'm afraid of like scared people."***
> Robert Frost

As can be seen, we are part of the same system and what we give out we in some way receive back. In bullying and harassing situations, it is particularly poignant and distressing that some people who are going through unhappy circumstances in their private lives seem to attract unpleasant behaviour at work. Instead of receiving support from their colleagues or managers, they get the opposite.

People who are under pressure and feeling vulnerable in one part of their lives may not have the resolve or confidence at that moment to deal with strong or difficult people at work. They may not have the strength to cope with an onslaught from every direction. Bullying becomes the last straw in a long and complicated catalogue of unhappiness.

> *When Martha came back from her maternity leave, her boss's attitude towards her seemed to change. She was tired and stressed about leaving her baby and the boss seized on her weak state. She became very depressed when he started making negative comments about working mothers and how their babies suffered. The criticisms he made of her work caused Martha to feel very upset and slowly her confidence in her abilities waned. This, in turn, reinforced his view that working mothers cannot cope.*

Pregnancy seems to be a catalyst for some people to experience unpleasant behaviour at work. Women often talk to me about the sexist comments they receive from their male colleagues about their health and appearance while pregnant. They are subject sometimes to demeaning and distasteful comments about breast feeding after they return from having babies. Many working mums report that their colleagues or managers believe they are no longer committed to their workload now they are mothers. They are accused of putting the needs of their family before the responsibilities of their job.

Behaviour and attitudes such as these from colleagues and managers can undermine women at a vulnerable stage in their working lives. As they show this vulnerability, they often either begin to attract even more undermining behaviour, or at least temporarily lose the ability to deal with it effectively. Their temporary weakness in some way compounds the unpleasant behaviour they are subject to. On the one hand, the bully seizes on this fragile state and, on the other hand, the recipient of this behaviour is unable to bounce back and deal effectively with it. One type of behaviour seems to lead to the other, and so the ripple goes on.

The women army officers quoted in Chapter 3 gave me a sad example of how vulnerability compounds vulnerability.

> *"A young woman officer was the only woman in a troop,"* according to a female colleague. *"She had nothing in her armoury to help her deal with being the only woman. She had low self-esteem that seemed to come from a poor relationship with her boyfriend, who was treating her badly. She did not stick up for herself. The men liked her, but subjected her to a lot of sexist banter and teasing. For them it was sport. She just took it and could not stand up to it. She became very depressed and had to have counselling. Yet when the men realised the effect their behaviour was having on her they were upset and tried to put matters right."*

There is no doubt that many women would find it difficult to be a woman alone in a troop of male army officers. However, in this young woman's case, she was less able to stand up for herself and deal with the male banter because of her vulnerable state caused by circumstances in her private life.

Another example of how hard it is for us to cope when we are weakened in some way was given by Teresa in Chapter 3.

> *"My self esteem was low when I left Sandhurst because I was injured. It took a good year to build myself up physically. When I got back into sport I was happier with myself. So during this period I was more fragile if someone shouted at*

me. But when I was fitter I was more confident, so I could deal with it better."

In this case, the young officer realised that her weakened physical state contributed to her lack of confidence. This meant she was less able to cope with authority and difficult situations. Her insecurity led to her becoming more vulnerable.

So far in this chapter we have discussed how we are a part of a larger system and that the behaviour of one person impacts upon another and vice versa. In bullying and harassing situations, unhappily an individual's vulnerability seems to compound the bad behaviour they are subject to. Does their weakness attract the bad behaviour or is it that their more vulnerable state prevents them from being resourceful in dealing with it? I think it is almost impossible to give a clear answer to this question.

It would be easy to blame the bully for picking on a weaker person. This statement has almost become a cliché when talking about bullying. However, I believe it is more helpful in dealing with bullying and harassment at work if we encourage the recipients to become resourceful so that they can challenge unacceptable behaviour in a way that is effective for themselves. If we ignore the part vulnerability plays in the system, we are tackling only a part of the problem.

In the workplace, we all have a role in supporting our colleagues if they are under stress. As managers, we should consider how far a member of staff's personal problems may be affecting their ability to act resourcefully. If we know of a colleague who is going through a bad patch, we should help them deal with strong characters at work who may be picking on them. We should assist them in challenging unpleasant and bullying attitudes and speak up on their behalf if we believe they are feeling too upset to do so for themselves. We should ask them what support they need and whether we can help them by encouraging them to talk through their difficulties.

> ***It was during those long and lonely years that my hunger for the freedom of my own people became a hunger for the freedom of all people, white and black. I knew as well as I knew anything that the oppressor must be liberated just as surely as the oppressed. A man who takes away another man's freedom is a prisoner of hatred, he is locked behind the bars of prejudice and narrow-mindedness. I am not truly free if I am taking away someone else's freedom, just as surely I am not free when my freedom is taken from me. The oppressed and the oppressor alike are robbed of their humanity.***[17]

We have established that we are part of a system and that our vulnerability can influence the amount of bullying we receive as well as the way we deal with it. Let's reflect for a moment on the person doing the bullying to see how far this person fits into this pattern.

We glibly talk about bullies and harassers. These are convenient words – a kind of shorthand or jargon that we understand and accept. But by using these terms, we are in danger of stereotyping all people who bully as monsters with horns growing out of their heads.

Some people do appear as monsters at times.

- The boss who bawls and shouts at his or her staff.
- The manager who makes unilateral decisions without considering the effect on others.
- Colleagues who gang up on an individual and make their life a misery.
- People who are sexist or racist to their staff or co-workers.

There are occasions when no member of staff can deal with behaviour such as this without the support of senior staff or supportive colleagues.

---

[17] Nelson Mandela, *Long Walk to Freedom*, Abacus, London, 1994.

However, when discussing bullying situations with people who have been on the receiving end of this type of behaviour, I often hear how it is not only the recipient of this behaviour who is feeling vulnerable. The bully may also be in a weakened state. His or her actions may appear tyrannical and unreasonable, but they may be the actions of a person who is feeling insecure and uncertain.

Again, I am not making excuses for bullying people. I am, however, applying the same theory to the bully as to the recipient – the bullies are part of a system too, and their vulnerability may be having a direct influence on their behaviour.

> *Sam put in a complaint of bullying against his line manager, James. He accused James of constantly criticising his work and undermining his confidence.*
>
> *James said Sam's work was below standard and offered Sam training to help him improve. Sam refused this and also refused to move to a section under another line manager so his situation could be reassessed impartially.*
>
> *James claimed that Sam began spreading stories about his management style, saying that James was not competent and shouldn't have been promoted. "I told him to stop saying this," said James, "as it was having an effect on me. I went through months of hell because of his attitude and I know this was influencing the way I treated him. Somehow it seemed to be working both ways. I was upsetting him and he was upsetting me."*

The more James upset Sam, the more Sam upset James. It would be difficult to decide which was the chicken and which the egg in this situation. Both people felt very unhappy and stressed and both believed the other person caused the misery. This is an example of the ripple effect, with the unhappiness of one leading to the suffering of the other.

Earlier in this chapter, Mary told us how her line manager bullied her and how she was sulky towards the manager in return. However, according to Mary, there was a possible reason for the manager's unpleasantness.

> *"My manager was having a bad time with a personal relationship," added Mary. "She was also doing exams and looking very stressed. In the end she was off ill for three months and then she resigned."*

In this situation, Mary's manager seemed to give out what she was receiving from others in her life. She was suffering in her personal life. She was under considerable stress. So she took it out on Mary. Or at the very least, she was feeling weakened by her own situation and so unable to deal effectively with Mary.

There were several missing ingredients in this situation which might have made a difference:

- Understanding by the manager of Mary's needs.
- Understanding by Mary of the stress her manager was going through.
- Support for Mary by her colleagues who were aware she was being picked on.
- Support for the manager by her more senior staff to help her through this difficult patch in her life.
- Training for the manager in people management skills – she was new to the post and it should have been someone's responsibility to make sure she was equipped with the necessary skills.

Modern workplaces often promote exceptional personal performers to positions of management over other staff. For example, engineers, technical staff, teachers, accountants, scientists – the list is endless – when they make their mark in an organisation, they may be rewarded by promotion. And along with this promotion comes responsibility for managing people.

What organisations seem to forget, however, is that excellent personal performers are not necessarily excellent people managers. People are not machines or financial targets, so why does it follow that if someone is an excellent inspector or technician, they are also equipped to supervise staff? Like any other role at work, people management requires training. Managers need support and guidance in dealing with their people management responsibilities.

Unless they are trained in dealing with people, coping with conflict, giving appraisals and feedback to staff and general interpersonal skills, how can we be sure that they will cope with these sensitive issues in a way that is both fair and supportive? Without this training, why are we surprised that managers resort to shouting, negative criticism, impatience and stereotyping – behaviour which by another name could be called bullying?

Any organisation that is serious about dealing with bullying and harassment should consider the way in which it promotes its staff into people management positions. It should then support those managers to enable them to deal fairly and effectively with the people under their command.

A quote from Helen Elaine Lee's *The Serpent's Gift* offers further insight into the mind of the bully. In this beautiful novel, the girl's father worked in the cotton fields in the Deep South of the USA in the late 19th century. He was always careful to show what he called 'proper respect' for his white master, while at the same time taking out his anger at his own position on his daughter.

> ***...(she) had always felt that her father had separated her out from the rest of the family as a focus for his rage. "You're headstrong and you'll never amount to anything," he had told her from the time she was a little girl, as if he hated her for her refusal to learn her place, for the resistance he could not afford in himself.***[18]

[18] Helen Elaine Lee, *The Serpent's Gift*, Scribner, New York, 1994.

To relate this to a workplace setting, it is worth considering that it is not only new managers who feel vulnerable. Even very senior managers with years of experience may not have the confidence we would expect.

> *Alex, a director of an organisation, was causing considerable distress to his team by his behaviour. He had a reputation as a bully and was well known by the staff as a very unpleasant character. He shouted at people during meetings, he threatened them with poor reports if they contradicted him, he rearranged their working loads deliberately to test them and he imposed unnecessarily harsh and unreasonable deadlines.*
>
> *All his team were afraid of him and no one would put in a complaint of bullying for fear of his retribution.*
>
> *His line manager, however, while accepting the fear Alex created, said he was a very different person at board meetings. He was almost obsequious in front of his more senior directors and behaved in a compliant and deferential way.*

So even the most senior bully may have a weak spot, a time or place in which he or she feels vulnerable and unsure. In the case of Alex, perhaps he was giving out what he was receiving. His obsequious behaviour in front of the more senior staff was a demonstration of his vulnerability. In turn, he was causing his staff to feel vulnerable by bullying them.

So this circuit goes on.

- We are part of the same system so we are liable to mete out what we receive from others.
- The bully is vulnerable so he or she takes it out on the staff.
- The member of staff is under some stress in another part of their life, so they are less able to cope with the bullying.

Thus the bullying continues until it gets out of hand or we change our response to it.

Hell and Heaven

A friend told me about a dream she had. She dreamt she died and went to hell.

"What was hell like?" I asked.

"Well," she said, "there was a large table in the centre full of the most delicious food you have ever seen. And people were walking all around it looking not only very miserable, but very thin and emaciated."

"Why were they not eating the lovely food?" I asked.

"They couldn't," my friend replied. "You see, their arms wouldn't bend at the elbows, so they couldn't get the food into their mouths. It really was an unpleasant sight.

"I woke up feeling quite unhappy and then drifted back into what I thought for a moment was the same dream. There was this table in the middle of the room full of delicious food. But I knew this must be heaven and not hell because the people were happy and smiling and looked very well fed."

"I suppose," I intervened, "that these people in heaven could bend their arms and so they could eat all they wanted."

"No," replied my friend, "they couldn't bend their arms, either."

"So how come they were so well fed and you knew this was heaven and not hell?" I asked.

"Well," said my friend, "they were feeding each other."

Exercise 8	**The miraculous circuit**
Think about a time when you were bullied. You may wish to reflect on the bullying you are experiencing at the present.	
List below the other things that were/are happening in your life that may have made/ be making you more vulnerable, *e.g. problems with a family member.*	**List below circumstances in the life of the bully that may have been/be influencing his or her behaviour and attitude,** *e.g. excessive pressure from a senior manager.*

Chapter 6

Navigating Stormy Seas

On the other side of what there isn't is what there is.[19]

We saw in Chapter 5 that we are part of a bigger system. Our behaviour impacts on other people, and their behaviour affects us. Whether we are being bullied, doing the bullying or are colleagues or managers of either party, we are to a greater or lesser extent involved with each other. We can change how we react to other people to encourage a different response from them. We can influence what is happening by supporting our colleagues, by challenging unreasonable behaviour and by contributing to a climate in which everyone is treated with respect.

Just as we are a part of the natural order of things, so too is conflict. Understanding that conflict is neither unnatural nor negative but just a normal occurrence helps us put it into perspective. It is not a weird phenomenon that strikes the unlucky like a bolt from the blue. Nor is it something that takes advantage of unsuspecting people, turning them into victims.

Thomas Crum explains this concept in his inspiring book *The Magic of Conflict:*

> ***... people come to me with conflicts they are having in their lives. It may be a relationship they are in, the type of work they do, a health problem, or a general dissatisfaction with their life. They inevitably speak of the conflict as bad: "I don't want it. I have to do something about it. It's harmful."***

---

[19] Helen Elaine Lee, *The Serpent's Gift*, Scribner, New York, 1994.

> ***... Nature doesn't see conflict as negative. Nature uses conflict as a primary motivator for change. Imagine floating down the Colorado River through the Grand Canyon. Quiet waters flowing into exhilarating rapids. Hidden canyons with shade trees and wildflowers. Clear springs of drinkable water. Solitude and silence that can be found in few places in today's world. And those majestic cliffs looming above, with fantastic patterns in the rock and all the colours of the rainbow displayed. The Grand Canyon is truly one of the world's great wonders and provides us with a profound sense of harmony and peace. Yet how was that amazing vista formed? Eons and eons of water flowing, continually wearing away the rock, carrying it to the sea. A conflict that continues to this day. Conflict isn't negative, it just is.***[20]

Crum's argument is that conflict is a natural occurrence. As in nature, there are times in our lives when we are in conflict situations. By accepting that 'conflict isn't negative, it just is', we can shed the feelings of guilt and inadequacy which we often suffer from when we face discord and disharmony. We have not failed because we encounter conflict in our lives. It is part of nature's motivator for change. Just as the waters of the Grand Canyon change the shape and size of the valley, so conflict in the workplace changes us all in many ways. We need to capitalise on these challenges and relish the opportunity for change that conflict gives us.

We discussed in Chapter 1 how damaging it can be to allow ourselves to take on a victim mentality if we are bullied or harassed. By so doing, we give the bully the opportunity to steal our power and resourcefulness. We become vulnerable, angry and resentful. Alice Walker points out the danger in feeling this way:

---

[20] Thomas Crum, *The Magic of Conflict, turning a life of work into a work of art*, Touchstone, New York, 1987.

Anger is great but it shouldn't be destructive. I feel lucky that, as a creative person, I can always build something rather than blow it up.[21]

Conflict is an opportunity to develop and change in a life-enhancing way. The women in the case studies in Chapter 3 remained on course, believing in themselves in spite of the negative behaviour they often faced. Carley, if you remember, did not allow the Detective Chief Inspector to turn her into a powerless victim by his sexist attitude. Remember what she said about him.

"I knew I could have got upset and been really damaged by his attitude. But I also knew I had to salvage my self-esteem, which was constantly in danger of being battered by him. So I thought, 'it's his problem not mine. It's his loss that he can't see women doing responsible jobs in the force. If he's going to go through life like that, then he's missing out on a lot.'"

Carley learned from the sexism and used it to develop her resolve. The conflict she faced encouraged her to grow stronger and she became even more determined to be successful in the police force.

Laura used the heated discussions with the boys in the pub to fine-tune the presentation of her arguments. Instead of losing her confidence when she was faced with their conflicting views, she learned how to match the boys' style of putting across their ideas. In this way she developed an expressive and forceful way of communicating her point.

Conflict, therefore, is both a natural phenomenon and a motivator for change. It offers us opportunities to learn, to grow and to become flexible in our responses to others. It gives us the chance to become more resourceful and to learn strategies to deal with difficult situations by ourselves or on behalf of other people.

[21] Alice Walker quoted in *The Guardian*, 29th April, 1998.

It is important to bear this in mind when faced with bullying or harassment at work. Instead of feeling victimised or damaged by the behaviour, we can choose to ask ourselves:

- **What can I learn from this conflict?**
- **What new resources within myself have I discovered from this conflict?**
- **In what ways have I grown as a result of this bullying?**

Conflict, such as bullying or harassment at work, gives us the possibility to learn about ourselves. It does not mean we have failed or are inadequate. It is an opportunity to develop and grow.

When we are faced with a bullying or harassing situation we should tell ourselves

This is a chance to learn, not a sign I have failed.

If we believe we have failed, we become the victim of the situation. We act in a negative way and think negative thoughts about ourselves and the other person involved. If, however, we accept that conflict is a natural part of our lives and an opportunity to learn, we increase the flexibility of our response to the person doing the bullying. We emerge from the situation more powerful than before.

It is interesting to reflect how we can learn from conflict. The following scenarios are examples of how three people used conflict to learn and change.

Scenario 1

My friend's teenage daughter is very uncommunicative first thing in the morning. She hardly speaks and only answers her mother in grunts and groans. My friend, however, is quite chirpy at breakfast time and feels upset when her daughter is monosyllabic and grumpy with her. Often this situation ends in a few cross words

and then they leave for work and college. My friend spends the day feeling unhappy about her relationship with her daughter and the daughter feels guilty about upsetting her mum.

Rather than thinking she has failed as a mother, what could my friend learn from this situation? The following are three possibilities:

✓ ***"My daughter, unlike myself, needs peace and quiet in the morning, so I will take my breakfast back to bed and leave her alone."***

✓ ***"I will watch breakfast television and not attempt to speak to my daughter unless she speaks first."***

✓ ***"I will discuss my feelings with her when she comes home from college this evening. I will explain my point of view and try to understand hers."***

Perhaps you could suggest more things that my friend could learn from this situation.

Scenario 2

Nancy decided to learn to drive when she was in her early 60s. Everyone said she would find it hard to pass the test at her age. She failed her first test and was subjected to "I told you so" from some of her friends.

Nancy could easily have decided she was too old to learn to drive and that she might as well give up trying. Or she could have chosen to learn one or all of the following from the situation:

✓ ***"I need to discuss my progress with my driving instructor and not listen to my friends."***

✓ ***"If I learn the Highway Code more thoroughly, I will feel more confident during my next test."***

✓ ***"My first test was a practice run from which I have learned X, Y and Z."***

Scenario 3

Tracey works as a secretary in an office of male technicians. This is her first job since leaving college. She finds it difficult to cope with the young technicians' sexist jokes and banter. It is worse when the boss is out of the office. There are no women on the staff to whom she can talk about this.

What could Tracey learn from this situation that will help her cope?

- ✓ ***"I could discuss this situation with my girlfriends outside work and ask them to help me prepare what I want to say to the men."***
- ✓ ***"The men are behaving in a very juvenile manner and I will not let them see that they upset me by doing this."***
- ✓ ***"I don't like working as the only woman in an office full of men, so I will look for a job where there are other women to work with."***

When we learn from a bullying or harassment situation, we increase our flexibility and our resourcefulness to cope with conflict now and in the future. Instead of allowing ourselves to feel that we have failed, we can learn from the events. By applying the belief that all situations and relationships offer us positive learning, we will grow in confidence rather than become ineffectual and powerless because of the actions of others.

Conflict can cause us to feel as if we are being tossed around by stormy seas. We feel helpless and at the mercy of others. However, when we are in a conflict situation, if we pause for a moment and reflect on what we can learn from this state of affairs, choices will appear. Instead of responding in an angry way or being incapable of taking action, we can consider what understanding we can gain from the conflict. In this way options will present themselves and we will begin to feel more resourceful. We can remind ourselves that we are not failures as people and that the feedback we are receiving from the other person is an opportunity for us to learn.

Learning is the key to using conflict as an opportunity to change. By reflecting on our feelings and actions and those of the other person involved we can learn how we might change our reactions to this person and how we can change our feelings about the difficult situation we are in.

We discussed in the last chapter that what we do has a ripple effect on other people. Remember the cliché, *It takes two to tango*? In any relationship with another person, we affect how they feel and behave and they affect us. If conflict occurs between us, we should remember that this is part of the natural order. Instead of taking on a victim-like stance and feeling that somehow we are failures, we can focus on the difficult relationship, consider what we can learn from this and how we can change our reactions to the other person.

When we become stressed by a difficult relationship, we tend to focus on the unacceptable behaviour we are enduring rather than noticing that what we are doing is having an effect on the situation too. We forget we can change what we do and how we respond to someone. When we are deeply involved in a conflict situation we lose our perspective on what is really happening and what we are doing.

How can we see things afresh so that we can learn how to change?

How can we begin to understand the other person's point of view and how we appear to them?

There are three ways of looking at a relationship. First of all, we can understand it from ***our own position.***

- We can see the other person.
- We can hear what they are saying and what we are saying.
- We can feel what we are feeling.

Secondly, we can try to understand it from the perspective of the ***other person.***

- We can reflect on what they see when talking to us and how we appear to them.
- We can reflect on what they hear when we are speaking to them.
- We can reflect on what they might be feeling when we are together.

Thirdly, we can try to understand what we would seem like if we were viewing the two of us from the viewpoint of ***a fly on the wall.***

- What does the fly see when the two of us are together?
- What does the fly hear?
- What does the fly notice about what we are feeling?

If we use this approach[22], we can learn so much about our relationship with the other person. As well as understanding our own point of view, we can begin to appreciate how we appear to other people and their different standpoint. We can spot what changes we may wish to make that will lead to an improvement in a relationship. These changes may involve:

- how we speak to the person,
- how we react to them,
- or how we feel about our relationship with them.

One or more of these changes may be sufficient to help us cope in a more resourceful way with this person. This in turn may cause a change for the better in how the person reacts to us.

---

[22] This technique is based on the NLP technique of Perceptual Positions clearly described in Sue Knight's book *NLP at Work*, Nicholas Brealey Publishing Ltd, London, 1995.

Elizabeth's relationship with her boss had changed recently. Previously, they had been on good terms and had an enjoyable working relationship. She knew her boss was a strong character who intimidated many of her colleagues, but she had always felt he treated her well and they could be frank and open with each other. In fact, she was quite relaxed in her dealings with him.

Things began to change and Elizabeth became very unhappy about this. It seemed to her that her boss had lost interest in her section and was no longer supporting her through difficult policy changes that were coming down from the board. She felt betrayed by his attitude. It seemed to her that he believed her section was dispensable now that it could no longer generate such a large profit for the organisation because of central policy decisions. She felt hurt by this and let down that all her previous hard work and commitment now seemed to mean nothing to him.

This deteriorating relationship came to a head one day when her boss called her in for a discussion of the situation. She felt apprehensive when she walked into his office as she knew he had a reputation for hard talking. Her fears were well founded for as soon as the meeting began, her boss began to give her a dressing down and criticised her attitude over the last few months. Elizabeth became very angry and the meeting degenerated into personal accusations and faultfinding. When she left his office, she felt their relationship had broken down irretrievably.

I encouraged Elizabeth to consider the unpleasant meeting again, this time trying to understand it through the perspective first of herself, then of her boss and then as a fly on the wall. I asked her to arrange the room so that she was sitting in approximately the same position as at the meeting and to imagine where her boss had been sitting.

She quickly recaptured her own feelings of this meeting – how she felt hurt and let down by her boss and how angry she had been when he started criticising her personally. She remembered how she had then started to criticise him personally and that from then onwards the meeting had become very unpleasant and unproductive. She described how powerful he appeared to her behind his big desk and how he had intimidated her, wagging his finger and raising his voice.

From Elizabeth's perception in this scenario, her boss had become a bully and was treating her as badly as he had treated some of her other colleagues. She felt very hurt by his attitude and angry that he had treated her in an unsupportive and aggressive way. She believed their good relationship had broken down completely and that there was little chance of repairing it.

Next I asked her to try to understand how this meeting had been from her boss's perspective. I asked her to change places and sit where her boss had been sitting. Obviously she could only guess what it had been like for her boss faced with this situation, but it was surprising how much she could conjecture.

She could see herself sitting in his office with a look, at first, of resentment at having been called to this meeting. She imagined how her boss might have been feeling confused by her reaction to him and disappointed in the breakdown of their good relationship. As she tried to see herself through her boss's eyes, she saw a strong and defiant woman who was stubbornly prepared to consider the situation only from her own point of view. Viewing the situation from his perspective, she saw the defiance in her own face when talking to her boss and she heard the personal criticisms she had put forward.

After this, I asked Elizabeth to pretend to be a fly on the wall and to describe herself and her boss in his office that day. She talked about two stubborn people who were aggressive and unrelenting towards each other. Both became angry and critical. Both had hostile body language that included finger wagging and irritable expressions on their faces. As the fly on the wall, Elizabeth heard loud voices and it seemed that neither party listened to the other. Each was so intent on making her or his point of view heard.

As Elizabeth went through this exercise she began to see things afresh. Her boss still appeared to her as a bully using aggressive language and being personally critical of her. However, she learned that her behaviour may have affected his attitude. During the exercise, she had seen herself taking a defiant stance and refusing to try to understand the situation from her boss's viewpoint. She now began to understand how she may have inflamed the situation, or at least aggravated it, by her attitude. She still felt her boss had been unsupportive towards her, but she realised that, because she had been angry and upset, she had not explained to him how she really felt. She had just countered each accusation with another accusation.

She began to realise that perhaps she had not listened to his side of the story. She had not taken into account the problems he might have been facing with the changes in policy that were coming from the board and that perhaps her defiant stance had been a threat to him. Indeed, she began to wonder whether they were both a threat to each other and that the behaviour of one had had a ripple effect on the other. It was almost impossible at this stage to say who had begun this ripple effect but it had gone out of control in such a damaging way that their relationship had broken down because of it.

From taking part in this exercise, Elizabeth learned that she had a strong effect on her boss and that she was not the poor victim she had first thought. Instead of feeling a failure she began to understand what she could do differently to try to repair the situation so that they could resume working together in an effective way. She knew that she needed to talk with her boss and explain how she felt about the way things had developed between them. She realised she needed to listen to his point of view and encourage him to listen to hers. From doing the exercise, she had learned that she could appear strong and powerful. What she needed to do was to consider how she could use this strength and power to begin to repair the relationship.

This exercise gave Elizabeth options that she had not had before. Previously, she had felt paralysed by the misery of the difficult situation she found herself in with her boss. She was hurt and angry and did not see why she had to do anything to make matters right. After all, she had thought, he was the boss and it was his fault he had not managed the situation better! He should know how to manage staff without bullying them.

Now she began to understand how her behaviour had impacted upon her boss. She had a sense of what he was feeling in this situation. She had no way of knowing if she had interpreted his point of view correctly, but at least she could begin to see what changes **she** might make to improve the situation.

- She could listen to her boss.
- She could explain her point of view.
- She could act less defiantly and angrily.

The choice was hers.

Native Americans have an expression that goes something like this:

> ***You cannot really understand me until you have walked a mile in my moccasins.***

If we are to truly understand the other person's point of view, we must step into their shoes and try to experience the world as if we were them. The understanding that follows is vital in influencing how we decide to deal with a harassment or bullying situation. Indeed, stepping into the other person's shoes may prevent a situation ending up as harassment or bullying. If we can second guess how a person feels or thinks and how we appear to them, we may be able to change what we do so as to create a more harmonious relationship. If Elizabeth had tried to see things from her boss's standpoint before this difficult meeting, things might not have gone so badly wrong.

Seeing things only from our own point of view can be damaging in working relationships. We can become so deeply entrenched in our own feelings that we forget to consider how we might appear to others. A recent employment tribunal case is a good example of this.

> *Two senior officers of a local authority ended up in court, with the female deputy accusing the male chief executive of sexually discriminating against her. The deputy complained there was an aggressive male culture in the council and a prevalent misogynist atmosphere. She spoke of incidents of physical sexual harassment and times when she was allowed less responsibility than men who were junior to her. Undoubtedly, from her point of view this was a very unpleasant situation to find herself in.*
>
> *However, when the chief executive spoke in court he denied bullying and humiliating his deputy. In contrast, he said the female deputy undermined and intimidated women officers and she had been aggressive and threatening towards him and her colleagues. The chief executive said he had asked her to show more respect to other members of staff.*

Often employment tribunals have to decide in cases like this who to believe and whether bullying or harassment has taken place. Yet, if these two people had been encouraged, before this situation ended up in court, to understand the effect their behaviour was having on each other and to step into the other's shoes for a little while, perhaps they could have found a way of working more effectively together. By going through the exercise of trying to see the other person's point of view and how their behaviour appeared to the mythical fly on the wall, perhaps they could have saved the council the half million pounds the case cost them. A simple enough way, I hear you saying, of saving money and angst.

The women in the case studies in Chapter 3 understood how their behaviour might affect men in the workplace. For example, Rachel said she had asked that the male officers did not stand up when she entered the room. "I didn't want the men to feel I was stopping them from behaving the way they usually did," she said. By considering their point of view, she prevented resentment building up between the male and female officers. Laura stated that when she was arguing with the boys in the pub that she accepted, "it is as important to listen to their point of view as it is to express my own." She was able to understand how they felt and how important it was to take their feelings into account.

If we consider our impact on other people and what impression we may be making on them we can give ourselves the opportunity to change what we do or say in order to create a different reaction from the other person. Like Elizabeth in the scenario above, we can reflect on bullying or harassing situations and consider how our behaviour and attitude might have appeared to others. We can step into their shoes for a moment and understand how they might have been feeling. We can reflect on what a fly on the wall might have noticed about our relationship.

We can see things afresh.

By so doing, we can give ourselves the opportunity to consider what changes we may wish to make to help improve the relationship or what support we may require from others. We can begin to feel resourceful once again and not victims of someone else's 'bad' behaviour. We can become **bully proof**.

We can drown in the stormy seas of conflict or navigate a safe course for ourselves.

The choice is ours.

The Story of the Two Villages

This is the story of two villages – one in the mountain and one in the valley. A traveller, walking along the road that linked the two villages, stopped to talk to a wise old woman leaning on a fence.

"Hello, wise old woman," said the traveller. "I'm on my way from the village in the mountain to the village in the valley. Could you tell me what the people in the village in the valley are like?"

"Of course I can, traveller, but first of all tell me, how did you find the people in the village in the mountain?"

"Oh, I'm glad to be leaving them," said the traveller. "They were very unfriendly and seemed suspicious of strangers. I didn't make any friends or get to know anyone. So I am keen to know what the people in the village in the valley are like."

"Well, traveller, you'll find them exactly the same."

The traveller wished the old woman goodbye and wearily went on his way.

The next day another traveller was walking along the road from the village in the mountain to the village in the valley when he spotted the wise old woman leaning on the fence.

"Hello, wise old woman," said the second traveller, "I've just left the village in the mountains and am travelling to the village in the valley. Do you know what the people are like in the village in the valley?"

"Indeed I do, traveller. But first of all tell me, how did you find the people in the village in the mountains?"

"Oh, I found them really pleasant. I've made a lot of friends and am sorry to be leaving them. So I am keen to know what the people in the village in the valley are like."

"Well, you'll find them exactly the same, traveller," said the wise old woman.

Exercise 9 Walking in their moccasins

You may wish to ask a friend to talk you through this exercise and then you could offer to do the same for them.

1. **Think of a time when you were in disagreement with someone at work or when you felt bullied or intimidated by another person.**
2. **Imagine where you and the other person were in the room. Arrange the furniture in a similar way if it helps.**
3. **First of all, sitting or standing in your position in the original incident, describe in the present tense what you can see, what the other person looks like, how they are sitting/standing, etc. Explain what you are feeling and what you are hearing. Take your time and fully associate into yourself in that situation.**
4. **Now shake off the feelings of yourself in the situation and walk around the room for a moment or two. When you are ready, sit or stand in the position of the other person. Try to put yourself in their position. As the other person, explain in the present tense what you see? Describe yourself from their perspective. Use the third person when talking about yourself and the first person when talking as if you were the other person. What do you hear? What do you feel?**
5. **Now shake off the feelings of the other person in the situation and walk around the room for a moment or two. When you are ready, take up the position a fly on the wall might have, i.e. distance yourself from the two people in the situation (yourself and the other person) and stand where you can imagine you can see them both. Describe them using the present tense. What do they look like together? What body language do you see? What are their facial expressions? How are they sitting or standing? What are they saying to each other? What do their voices sound like? What do you imagine they are feeling?**

6. **Now shake off the feelings of being the fly on the wall and when you are ready, think what you have learned from being in the three positions above. Complete the following:**

   I now know the following about myself in this situation

   I now know the following about the other person in this situation

   I can now react differently to this other person or think differently about them by

   I now need to

Chapter 7

Taking the Plunge

It is better to have lived one day as a tiger, than one thousand years as a sheep. Tibetan Proverb

So far we have seen that when facing unacceptable behaviour in the form of bullying or harassment at work we do not need to remain powerless victims. Instead, we can choose to feel resourceful and strong. We can choose to react in a way that leaves us feeling comfortable and sure that what we did was right for us. In other words, we can become **bully proof**.

Earlier chapters pointed out a range of key factors that contribute to this resourcefulness.

- We don't have to do what we have always done in conflict situations. We can choose to make changes. We discussed how we cannot make another person change no matter how much we may wish to do so. We do not have the power to do this. We do, however, have the power to change our reactions to the other person which in turn may cause them to react differently. This is our strength and we should use it.
- We can also choose to change how we perceive people and situations. Reality is not set in stone. My reality is not the same as yours. At some level, I have chosen to make it the way it appears to me. Similarly, I can choose to change it. Remember how we could change our reality as children? What is stopping us from doing it now?
- We saw how some women when faced with male dominated working cultures choose to stay on course, believing in themselves. They hold empowering beliefs in

their strengths and capabilities. They understand how they are perceived by others and, to a certain degree, match their behaviour and approach to that of the other person. However, they stay true to themselves no matter what conflict or unpleasantness they face. They maintain an inner belief in themselves.

- We discussed how we can all use this strategy for staying on course, believing in ourselves and how each of us has such a successful strategy which we can use when we choose to do so. However, none of us are islands and, just as a stone thrown into a pond makes ripples, so our behaviour impacts on others. Not only does the bully's behaviour affect us, so too does our behaviour affect the bully.
- We considered how conflict is a natural phenomenon and that when we are faced with it we should not consider ourselves failures. Instead, we can view conflict as an opportunity to learn and develop. By understanding the other person's point of view, we can learn how we impact upon them. When we have this knowledge, a range of choices is opened up to us – choices that suggest ways we can go forward feeling resourceful and powerful once again.

One very important step we may wish to take when confronted by unacceptable behaviour in the workplace is to challenge this unacceptable behaviour and confront the person who is doing this to us. Instead of tolerating the behaviour and allowing it to continue without making our point of view known, we may decide to react in a different way and challenge the person concerned. We may decide to tell them how we feel and ask them to stop doing what it is that is causing us to feel unhappy, angry or distressed.

At times, we may feel overwhelmed by the prospect of taking the plunge and challenging the unacceptable behaviour. Indeed, there may be times when we know it is safer for us to let the bad behaviour pass. We should always put our personal safety and survival at the top of our list of priorities. If by confronting a bully we feel we will place ourselves in physical danger then, of course, we should avoid this at all costs. In circumstances such as these we may wish to ask for help from someone in a more powerful position than ourselves. This could be a more senior manager or personnel officer.

Putting ourselves in a confrontational situation may bring back memories of when we tried to do this in the past and the situation became worse. We can all remember times when we decided to speak to someone regarding something we felt very strongly about and the end result was unsatisfactory. We lost our tempers, said things we later regretted, or burst into tears and were unable to say what we really felt. In other words, we dived in and made matters worse.

No one can guarantee that the other person will not get angry and unpleasant. If you feel genuinely frightened of this person, then under no circumstances should you approach them alone. Take a witness in the form of a friend with you for moral support. Ask a colleague or a more senior member of staff to talk to the person on your behalf.

However, in many situations you will feel you want to talk to the person and try to create the working environment you desire and deserve. If you are to demonstrate your new resourceful state and the fact that you have thrown off the victim-stance, it is important that you feel confident in doing this. Likewise, you may need to consider the best way of approaching a manager or personnel officer to support you, but may not know how to go about this.

Rather than feel daunted at the prospect, reassure yourself that you already have the resources to do it. It isn't a case of learning a newfangled way of doing things. The approach I suggest allows you to capitalise on your own resources and ensures that you will do and say things in a way that is true to yourself. No matter what the outcome, afterwards you will feel strong in the belief that you did what was right for you and you did it in a way that was congruent with how you feel and who you are.

We have discussed the main components of this approach in previous chapters, but let's put them all together to make a Communication Model that is right for you.

> ***What an amazing world it would be if, when we receive hurt from another, we did not lash out but responded only when we were clear about what would be healing to the other and to ourselves.***[23]

This model is made up of three components:

1. Permission

How often, when we are upset or angry about something or someone, a well-intentioned friend or colleague says, "Well, I think you should tell him X," or "If I were you, I wouldn't stand for that, I'd do Y." They then proceed to give you lots of 'good' advice and walk away feeling pleased they could help you.

You, on the other hand, feel even more confused. Although you may have told your self-appointed helper you agreed with them, you are not sure that their approach suits you. You know deep down that their way is not your way and you do not believe that this approach will be successful. You are reluctant to do what they say as it doesn't feel right for you. You may even decide to do nothing now as you feel perplexed and weighed down by their good intentions.

In turn, we have often tried to help someone by suggesting what they should do and telling them how we dealt with a similar situation in the past. In other words, we told them *our* way of doing it. However, we are all different. We each see, hear and feel differently about the same situation. There may be some similarities in our reactions, but I can never be sure that you appreciate something in exactly the same way I do, and vice versa.

---

[23] Anne Wilson Schaef, *Native Wisdom for White Minds*, Ballantine Books, New York, 1995.

Consequently, my telling you what you should do may not be helpful. What may help you more would be if I encouraged you to think through which approach is right for you – the one that would make you feel the most comfortable and sure that you have taken the right action.

The subjects of the case studies in Chapter 3 carried some empowering beliefs that helped them be sure that their way was right for them. The most potent of these was:

It's OK to be me.

If you truly take on this belief, you will give yourself permission to do what is right for you, knowing that your way is fine. You don't have to adopt the style of another person or speak the words that they say are correct. It's perfectly OK to feel the way you do and to want to challenge this unacceptable behaviour in a way that is right for you.

In Exercise 7, you determined your own values – the core criteria that are the basis upon which you judge your actions and those of others. In Chapter 4, we discussed how the women who stayed on course, believing in themselves, were aware of the values they held. For example, Sarah said if she was not treated with **respect** she knew she had the right to object to someone's behaviour or withdraw from a situation. By noting that a core value or criteria had not been met, she gave herself **permission** to do something about it.

Likewise, you can give yourself permission to take action by checking out your core criteria. If these criteria are not being met, you know you are right to speak up for yourself.

> *Joanna and her colleagues have been working extremely hard on a new project for the last few weeks. They worked late on many occasions and came in on a couple of Saturdays to use the computer equipment. This weekend Joanna's daughter is coming home for the weekend and she wants to spend as much time as possible with her.*
>
> *Her colleagues, however, intend to work on the project over the weekend and expect Joanna to do the same. One of*

Joanna's core values is ***to look after herself****. She knows if she doesn't do this, she gets tired and resentful of others and she is unable to help other people as well as she would like.*

Knowing this gives her the permission to say to her colleagues that this weekend she is unable to work on the project. She feels comfortable saying this clearly and calmly knowing that, by doing so, she is being true to herself. By spending a relaxing weekend with her daughter, she can meet her core value of looking after herself. Working on the project will go against this criterion. So she does not have to look further for permission to state her refusal. She gives herself this permission.

By checking on your core values, you know that if they are not being met, you have your own permission to do or say something that is right for you. By being true to yourself in this way, you will not be a victim to others. You will feel resourceful and sure of yourself. You will know what is right for the unique you that you are. In other words, it is OK to be you.

2. Actively seek to understand

When challenging unacceptable behaviour and attitudes, you are seeking to influence the other person involved. You want the chance to tell the other person how you feel, but you also want to influence them in some way. You want to encourage them to stop doing that which you find unacceptable and to start treating you with respect.

In our everyday lives, we are influenced by many factors. These include advertising and economics, as well as behaviour and emotions such as threats, love, compassion and fear. We are each, however, influenced by these factors in different ways.

- An advertising campaign for a small but powerful sports car might influence me but not you, especially if you have five children and two large dogs to transport around.
- If you threatened to thump me I might be terrified, but if you threatened to thump a world champion boxer he is unlikely to be overly concerned.

These are obvious examples – sports car manufacturers understand which people will be attracted by their campaigns and you can easily understand how influential the threat of violence would be to me as opposed to a burly boxer. In everyday communication, however, it may not be so easy to understand the person we are talking with, or to be sure we can influence them.

In the last chapter, we spent some time considering how to see a situation or a relationship from the other person's perspective. We set out to understand their point of view and to see the world from their position. We tried walking in their moccasins for a little while to comprehend more fully how we appeared to them and what they might be feeling and thinking.

When viewing the situation from the other person's perspective, we do not need to agree with them. Sometimes the behaviour of a bully may still be totally unacceptable to us even when we have tried to embrace their standpoint.

However, if we are to influence them, we need to try to understand them and to acknowledge this understanding. No matter how unreasonable another person's attitude may seem to us, their attitude is theirs at this moment. It may seem very wrong to us, but we need to acknowledge that they hold it if we are to seek to influence them. If we do not, our relationship will continue to be similar to two bulls with their horns locked in conflict.

3. Communicate empathically

When we have actively sought to understand the other person and have acknowledged their point of view, we are beginning to communicate empathically with them.

Empathy is the power of understanding and the ability of entering into another person's feelings. When we communicate empathically, we demonstrate we understand their point of view and their right to hold it. It does not mean that we agree with their point of view, only that we acknowledge it.

The women in Chapter 3 who stayed on course, believing in themselves, had an awareness of the viewpoints of the men they were working with. Laura knew that the men did not value an emotional style of discussion. Laura matched their style when arguing with them over women's football. This did not mean that Laura agreed that a more impassionate, logical style is the best one to have. It meant that Laura communicated empathically with the men. She matched their more masculine and logical style of discussion to influence their point of view. She understood what they believed in. She was able to relate to them in a way that demonstrated that she recognised what they valued. In other words, she was communicating empathically with them.

If Laura had not actively sought to understand the men with whom she was talking, she would have been unlikely to have spoken with them in an influential way. Instead, like some of her girl friends, she would have been subject to the verbal abuse or banter that they found unacceptable. From then onwards, it would have been easy to degenerate into personal attacks and criticisms.

The key ingredients of communicating empathically, therefore, are:

- Acknowledging the other person's point of view.
- Matching their style as far as we can, while at the same time remaining true to ourselves.
- Not being drawn into personal criticisms, only challenging the person's behaviour.

The last point is very important. We have noted on several occasions that one person's reality is not necessarily shared by others, that we each see the world from our own perspective. We may not agree with another person's way of doing things, but for some reason, their way is right for them at that moment. However unpleasant another person may seem to us, we should remember that a bully is not necessarily a bad person, just a person behaving badly. It is their behaviour we are objecting to;

not them as human beings. We are not out to damage or destroy them – instead we are intent on influencing them.

These are the three key ingredients of the Communication Model – ingredients that you already possess and can use resourcefully when you choose.

You may have noticed that I have not given you a script to follow when challenging unacceptable behaviour. I have not said that if you just say X or Y, all will be OK. I believe that if you follow this Communication Model you will not need to be told what to say. When you have:

- Given yourself **permission** to speak out against unacceptable behaviour by taking on the empowering belief that **It's OK to be me** and checked this out with your core criteria, and
- **actively sought to understand** the other person by seeing the situation from their point of view and acknowledging their right to have feelings and hold certain opinions, then you will be ready to
- **communicate empathically** with the other person. You will match their style as far as is appropriate for you and feel resourceful in saying what you know you need to say in a way that allows you to remain true to yourself.

You may find it helpful to ask a friend to coach you through this model, or you may wish to spend some time alone preparing yourself. If you use a friend in this way, don't forget you are asking them to coach you through it. You are not asking them to tell you what to say or what they would say in your position.

Remember, **you have the resources to do this in a way that is right for you**. By using this model, you will harness those resources and speak in a way that is powerful and true to you.

> ***It's not whether you have conflict in your life. It's what you do with that conflict that makes a difference... Resolving conflict is rarely about who is right. It is***

about acknowledgement and appreciation of differences.[24]

Let's consider how this communication model opens up choices.

Trevor works as a middle manager in a large organisation. George, his senior manager, holds monthly meetings during which Trevor presents his section's monthly report. Two months ago, George had been impatient with Trevor and had interrupted him on a couple of occasions during his presentation. At last month's meeting, Trevor found George's attitude towards him hostile and unpleasant. George did not appear to listen to Trevor's report and addressed angry comments at him in front of the full team. Trevor tried to discuss the points George was raising calmly and clearly but, as he did so, George became even more irritable towards him. In the end Trevor felt he had no choice but to remain silent and suffer the humiliation of George's angry tirade.

How could the Communication Model help Trevor?

First of all, he considered giving himself **permission** to speak to George outside the meeting. He placed great value on happiness – working and living in an environment where he found pleasure and comfort. Since George's outbursts against him, these core criteria were not being met. Trevor was not deriving pleasure or happiness from work. By taking on the belief that it was OK to be him, he told himself it was right for him to speak to George about this.

Secondly, he **actively sought to understand** George in this situation by going through the exercise of trying to see things from George's point of view. Trevor already knew that during the meeting he felt humiliated and very uncomfortable. George appeared angry and impatient with him. When he tried to see things from George's point of view, he began to realise that

---

[24] Thomas Crum, *The Magic of Conflict, turning a life of work into a work of art*, Touchstone, New York, 1987.

George liked quick and brief presentations and was feeling very impatient with Trevor's more reflective and wordy approach. When he tried to view himself through George's eyes, he saw a rather determined person who was not going to alter his style to suit George and the pressures George was under at present. And as the fly on the wall, Trevor saw two people whose body language demonstrated discomfort, dislike and lack of concern each for the other.

Thirdly, he considered how he could **communicate empathically** with George. He was now recognising that George had a quick and rather abrupt style, in contrast to his own slower, more pensive one. He also began to realise the pressures George may be under from other parts of the department as well as those from Trevor's section. This could explain his impatience and irritability. He also took into account that on Friday afternoons George was often cheerful and quite jovial as he looked forward to a weekend away from the office.

Trevor realised after going through the model that he had choices in what he could do to bring about changes in the difficult situation he found himself in. Feeling confident that, by checking on his beliefs and values, he had given himself permission to challenge George, he began to consider how he could do so in a way that matched George's quick style. He spent some time thinking through what he wanted to say and then practised saying it to himself in as brief a way as possible. He wrote a short note to George and asked to see him on Friday at 4.30pm.

When Friday afternoon came Trevor knew that he was prepared for this meeting with George. He felt sure that it was right for him to talk to George and was clear in what he wanted to say and the way in which he would say it. Whatever the result of this meeting, he knew he would feel certain that he had done what was right for him in an attempt to improve this unacceptable situation.

This Communication Model gives you choices. Instead of being paralysed by the unacceptable behaviour of another person, by going through the model you can find a resourceful way forward. You will know that you have considered the perspective of the person who is behaving badly and sought an empathetic way to communicate with her or him. Above all the choices will be congruent with your beliefs and values. This congruence will ensure that what you say and how you say it will be the right way for you. And you will demonstrate to yourself and to others that you are **bully proof**.

A Jewish Search

There was once a young man of the Synagogue of Cracow. He knew that he was fortunate and had much to be happy about; but he was haunted by a great question. With all that he had been given what should he do with his life? No one in his synagogue could help, but some said the Librarian at Prague was sure to know.

So he made the long journey to Prague. It was autumn, the rain soaked him and the roads were mostly black mud, but he pressed on. And the Librarian at Prague told him that what he must do with his life was study. So the young man tried it, but it didn't satisfy him and every time he looked round the endless shelves heavy with books, his heart quailed. How could he ever finish such a task?

Then someone told him of the Hermit at Lubov, so he went there. Autumn had turned to winter, the wind howled round his ears and his face froze as he trudged through the snow, but he pressed on. And the Hermit told him that what he must do with his life was meditate. So the young man tried it, but it didn't satisfy him, and he felt his life was slipping away in the solitude.

He tried many masters after that. His feet came to know the roads of Europe and he heard advice in many languages from the lips of many gurus. But the question still stayed with him; with all that he had been given, what must he do with his life?

Then, in a town like many others, a peasant woman told him to seek the Rabbi Jonas Lieb, who would surely be able to help. So he set out one more time. It was high summer. The sun scorched his skin, the flies were a torment, the place was remote and the paths stony. But finally he found the Rabbi Jonas Lieb, living in a shack in a little village among the poorest people. And the old Rabbi listened carefully to the young man's story. Then, after a silence, he spoke.

"When I was young," he said, "I was troubled by exactly the same question, but then I had a dream. I dreamed that I had died and I was going up into heaven. I was terrified! I knew what they would ask me; Jonas Lieb, with all that you were given, why were you not another Moses? Or another Elijah? And I had no answer!

"So up I went, through great clouds that blazed with light and were filled with the incense of heaven and the songs of the blessed. And sure enough, I came face to face with the great angel. But he did not ask what I expected. He asked, "With all that you were given, why were you not Jonas Lieb?"

Exercise 10	**Taking the plunge**
Think about a situation where you would like to speak out resourcefully and challenge the behaviour of another person.	
1. Permission	Refer back to your core values from Exercise 7. In what ways does this behaviour go against your values? How are your values not being met by this behaviour? Take on an empowering belief such as: It's OK to be me and to feel the way I do about this situation.
2. Actively seek to understand	Thinking about the key person involved in the situation go through Exercise 9 and try to understand what is happening from this other person's perspective and from that of a fly on the wall. List below: Their feelings towards you. How you appear to them. What you have learned from being a fly on the wall in this situation.
3. Communicate empathically	What are the key differences between your communication style and that of the other person? How could you match that person in a way that will help you communicate empathically with them? Are there any small changes you could make to your communication style that will help you appear empathic to the other person?

Chapter 8

Full Steam Ahead

> ***People travel to wonder at the height of the mountains, at the huge waves of the sea, at the vast compass of the ocean, at the circular motion of the stars and they pass themselves by without wondering.*** St Augustine

If meaningful change in the workplace is to take place, people on the receiving end of harassment and bullying need more than organisation policies and procedures to help them deal with unacceptable behaviour. Despite the attempts of well meaning organisations to address the problem, the number of people reporting cases or seeking help remains pitifully low. People are reluctant to submit complaints about harassment and bullying for many reasons, including fear of retribution from the bully or belief that nothing will be or can be done to help them.

Although organisational support is the first step in creating workplaces where everyone is treated with dignity, this alone is not enough. The significant change will come when employees:

- stay on course, believing in themselves so that they are not damaged or made to feel inadequate by the behaviour of others, and when they
- feel resourceful enough to challenge unacceptable behaviour in a way that is right for them.

We need to understand that there are choices we can make when faced with bullying and harassment at work. The first choice is to decide to throw off the victim-like stance that unacceptable behaviour at work can cause.

No one can make you feel inferior without your consent.
Eleanor Roosevelt

We can choose to feel resourceful, we can change how we allow situations to affect us, and we can do something different in order to create a different reaction from the bully or harasser.

No one should feel alone in making these choices. As managers and colleagues, we each have a responsibility to support our co-workers as they strive to become resourceful. We are each part of a system – not isolated and unaccountable for the effect we have on others and what is happening to our colleagues. We have an important role to play to ensure that unacceptable behaviour is not tolerated and that no one feels alone or betrayed.

Allan is a police constable who has been in the force for 20 years. On his section is a young black female recruit. She is the only black officer in the station and is the only female on the section. Allan told me how she is the subject of sexist and racist jokes from the white male officers. According to Allan, the joking is relentless and has been going on for some time. "I don't know how she puts up with it," says Allan. "I find it offensive so I am sure she must. I can't understand why she doesn't say something to them."

So here he is, Allan, a middle-aged constable with years of experience behind him – experience which in the police force is often as important as rank as far as influence over other police officers is concerned. Yet he has said nothing about the sexist and racist jokes a young black female recruit has to endure. Not only that, he wonders why she hasn't said anything about it herself.

Why doesn't he realise how difficult it must be for her, a young black woman alone with these men, to speak out for herself? Why doesn't he challenge the other officers himself on her behalf or check out with her what support she would like to help her deal with this situation? Why doesn't he do something different to ensure this young woman is treated with respect and becomes more resourceful?

Until we each play our part in dealing with harassment and bullying in the workplace, change will not occur. We should not bury our heads in the sand or leave it up to the person at the receiving end of the unacceptable behaviour to do something about it. We each have a responsibility to create a workplace where everyone is treated with respect.

This book has suggested that there are choices we can make when supporting others or dealing with harassment and bullying at work for ourselves. We have discussed how conflict is a natural part of our lives and that we should use it as an opportunity to learn. We can choose to make changes that will help us or our colleagues feel powerful. The choice is ours.

As you worked through this book I am sure you began to see how you can change your reality and feel resourceful once more or support your colleagues in doing this – how you and they can become **bully proof**. As you continue to do this, the following checklists will be a useful reminder of the strategies you are using.

Staying on course, believing in yourself

1. Take on an empowering belief

Presuppose you carry one or all of the following empowering beliefs:

- It's OK to be me.
- I believe in myself even if others don't.
- I know I am good at what I do.
- I believe others are just as interested in my point of view as they are in their own.
- I have the right to say what I think.
- I know when something is right for me.

Remind yourself of these beliefs each time you are faced with unacceptable behaviour. Experience the power these beliefs give you.

2. Check that your core values are being met

Understand your core values – they are fundamental to the way you are in the world. They are yours and no one can take them away from you. Whenever you feel uneasy or unhappy about the behaviour of another person, check out your core values. If one of them is not being met by the situation you are facing, then you know you have the right to do something to change the situation. Choices will appear for you.

3. Check out what is right for you

You know when something is making you feel unhappy. You know when your core values are not being met. If at the same time you take on the empowering belief that **It's OK to be me**, you will be sure that it is right for you to challenge the unacceptable behaviour or to do something different to create a change in the situation. Check with your feelings. You have the answer within.

4. Match the other person

Try to understand the style of the other person and find some way of matching that style. Make sure, however, that you stay within the boundaries you have set for yourself and only behave in a way that is congruent with your own core values.

5. Take on a powerful representation of yourself

Remember your metaphor for yourself. It may be an animal or bird. It may be a strong image or sound. Whatever it is, it is yours. You carry this with you. Bring it into your mind when you are facing difficult situations. Take on this powerful representation and notice how you take on feelings of resourcefulness and confidence.

Even when you are staying on course, believing in yourself, there may be times when you need to challenge unacceptable behaviour either on your own behalf or on behalf of colleagues. The following model allows you to do this.

Challenging unacceptable behaviour – taking the plunge

1. Give yourself permission

Remind yourself that **It's OK to be me** and check whether your core values are being met. If not then you have your own permission to challenge the unacceptable behaviour.

2. Actively seek to understand

Understand the other person's point of view as far as you possibly can. Go through Exercise 9 ***Walking in their moccasins***. Acknowledge your understanding of their position.

3. Communicate empathically

Match the other person's style as far as is congruent with your own beliefs and values. Tell them you find their behaviour unacceptable **not** them as people. Do this in a way that allows you to stay true to yourself and to use your own unique resources.

Use these checklists to remind yourself that

- You can learn from every situation and change your reality accordingly.
- You can change your reactions to another person.
- You are part of a system and what you do has an effect on others.

You have the resources to stay on course, believing in yourself and to challenge unacceptable behaviour. You can become bully proof.

Remember – the choice is yours.

A Snowflake

"Tell me the weight of a snowflake," a small bird asked a wild dove.

"Nothing more than nothing," was the answer.

"In that case, I must tell you a marvellous story," the small bird said. "I sat on the branch of a fir, close to its trunk, when it began to snow – not heavily, not in a raging blizzard – no, just like in a dream, without a wind, without any violence. Since I did not have anything better to do, I counted the snowflakes settling on the twigs and needles of my branch. Their number was exactly 3,741,952. When the 3,741,953rd dropped onto the branch, nothing more than nothing as you say, the branch broke off."

Having said that, the small bird flew away.

The dove, since Noah's time an authority on the matter, thought about the story for a while, and finally said to herself, "Perhaps there is only one person's voice lacking for peace to come to the world."

Appendix

Definitions

Sexual Harassment

The European Commission offers an excellent definition of sexual harassment:

> *"Sexual harassment means unwanted conduct of a sexual nature or other conduct based on sex affecting the dignity of women and men at work. This can include unwelcome physical, verbal or non-verbal conduct."*

The Equal Opportunities Commission in the UK recommends this definition and many companies, local authorities and government departments and agencies use it in their equal opportunities policies.

The term 'unwanted' is important as it means that it is up to the person on the receiving end of harassment to define unwanted and not for the organisation or any other person to do so. Consequently, what is not deemed as unwanted by a group of people may be unwanted by one person; for example, a woman working in a mainly male section.

Conduct of a sexual nature or other conduct based on sex could include any of the following:

- casual touching
- suggestive or over-familiar behaviour
- display or circulation of sexually suggestive material
- innuendo, foul language, lewd remarks, and the general use of provocative language

- sexually explicit talk, blue jokes or insensitive pranks
- comments on a woman's or man's physique
- unwelcome, persistent questioning about a woman's or man's personal life.

Sexual harassment has been held to constitute direct discrimination on the grounds of sex under the Sex Discrimination Act (1975 as amended).

Racial Harassment

It is unlawful under the Race Relations Act (1976) in the UK to discriminate directly or indirectly against individuals on the grounds of:

- colour
- race
- nationality
- ethnic or national origins.

Although not specifically mentioned in the Act, racial harassment is taken by employment tribunals to be direct discrimination that may take the form of behaviour of a racist nature such as:

- physical abuse
- offensive or abusive racist remarks
- racist jokes or graffiti
- derogatory comments about accent or manner of speech
- exclusion from conversations or particular types of work
- pressure about the speed and quality of work
- unfair work allocation
- silence towards the person.

Disability Harassment

Although not specifically stated, disability harassment is deemed to come under the Disability Discrimination Act (1995).

Disability harassment is directed at staff with disabilities or specific health conditions. It includes behaviour towards a disabled person such as:

- less favourable treatment
- offensive or patronising remarks
- ridicule
- exclusion from certain types of work
- ignoring or devaluing ability
- physical assault
- restricted work opportunities
- excluding the employee from conversations or full participation at work
- victimisation for challenging these actions and behaviours.

Bullying

Unlike the three forms of harassment above, bullying is not included in discrimination legislation. Consequently, individuals have little legal protection against bullying. An employee can claim constructive dismissal on the grounds that bullying involves a breach of mutual trust and confidence between the employee and the employer. However, to do this you must have two years' service and resign. An employment tribunal would hear the case and the maximum award would be the same as for all constructive dismissal cases, approximately £12,000.

However, if a claim for bullying was made under Health and Safety legislation and it was found that stress had occurred as a result of the bullying, there would be no ceiling to the award and no length of service requirement, as in discrimination cases.

Many organisations include bullying in their equal opportunities policies and the definitions that are used are generally along the lines of the following:

Intimidation or belittling of someone through the misuse of power or position, which leaves them feeling hurt, humiliated, vulnerable or powerless. This behaviour can take any of the following forms:

- behaviour which is offensive, abusive, intimidating or demeaning, or verbal or physical intimidation
- behaviour which is malicious or insulting or unjustified criticism
- sanctions imposed without reasonable justification
- changes in the duties or responsibilities of the employee to the employee's detriment without reasonable justification.

The author strongly recommends that anyone who believes they are being harassed or bullied at work seeks advice from a trade union or Personnel department before embarking on litigation.

The following addresses may be useful for people who need advice.

Equal Opportunities Commission	Overseas House Quay Street Manchester M3 3HN Tel: 0161 833 9244
Equal Opportunities Commission for Northern Ireland	22 Great Victoria Street Belfast BT2 7BA Tel: 01232 242752

Commission for Racial Equality

Elliot House
10-12 Allington Street
London
SW1E 5EH
Tel: 0171 828 7022

Commission for Racial Equality Northern Ireland

Scottish Legal House
65-67 Chichester Street
Belfast BT1 4JT
Tel: 01232 315996

Fair Employment Commission
For religious and political discrimination in employment, Northern Ireland only

Andras House
60 Great Victoria Street
Belfast
BT2 7BB
Tel: 01232 240020

The Royal Association for Disability and Rehabilitation (RADAR)

12 City Forum
250 City Road
London EC1V 8AF
Tel: 0171 250 3222
Minicom: 0171 250 4119

Stonewall
Working for lesbian and gay equality

16 Clerkenwell Close
London EC1R 0AA
Tel: 0171 336 8860

References

The following publications are referred to in this book and I am grateful to the respective publishers and authors for permission to reproduce extracts of their work:

Coelho, Paulo, *The Alchemist*, Harper Collins Publishers, London, 1995.

Crum, Thomas, *The Magic of Conflict, turning a life of work into a work of art*, Touchstone, New York, 1987.

Jeffers, Susan, *End the Struggle and Dance with Life*, Hodder and Stoughton, London, 1997.

Keenan, Brian, *An Evil Cradling*, Vintage, London, 1992.

Knight, Sue, *NLP at Work*, Nicholas Brealey Publishing Ltd, London, 1995.

Lee, Helen Elaine, *The Serpent's Gift*, Scribner, New York, 1994.

Mandela, Nelson, *Long Walk to Freedom*, Abacus, London, 1994.

Michaels, Anne, *Fugitive Pieces*, Bloomsbury Publishing Plc, London, 1997.

Whitefield, C.L., *Healing the Child Within*, Health Communications, Orlando, Florida, 1989.

Wilson Schaef, Anne, *Native Wisdom for White Minds*, Ballantine Books, New York, 1995.

Jean Kelly is a leading trainer and consultant in the field of combating harassment and bullying at work. Her company, Jean Kelly CONSULTANCY, pioneers the Bully Proof © approach to dealing with unacceptable behaviour at work by running small workshops and individual coaching sessions. Jean has a Masters Degree in Gender and Education and is a Master Practitioner of Neuro-Linguistic Programming.

Jean Kelly CONSULTANCY

Coaching

- One-to-one sessions with all parties involved in harassment and bullying incidents.
- **Bully Proof** © coaching for recipients of harassment.
- Coaching for alleged bullies and harassers to help them reassess their behaviour and review its impact on others.

Consultancy

- Research into the extent of bullying and harassment in the workplace.
- Equality Audits to evaluate the effectiveness of equality policies and to address the under-representation of minority staff in the workplace.

Training

- **Bully Proof** © Workshops.
- Awareness Raising of the legal and workplace consequences of harassment and bullying, for managers, teams and personnel.
- Senior Management Briefings in combating harassment and bullying.
- Harassment Adviser Training which includes listening skills development and defining roles and procedures.
- Investigating Cases of Harassment and Bullying Skills Training for managers.
- Away Days for Teams to help them develop effective team relationships.

All training custom-designed
to meet organisational needs

For full details contact

Jean Kelly CONSULTANCY

Garth End
Church Road
Farnham Royal
Buckinghamshire
SL2 3AW

Email: Jeank232@aol.com